ACKNOWLEDGEMENTS

A huge thank you to Della Rounick! Della, your dazzling personal savvy, glamorous fashion style and elegant global lifestyle has, over the many valued years of our friendship, taught me what being a real Glamazon is about!

A big Glama thank you to Patsy Rowe—always a total Glamazon from top to toe. Patsy, your presence in my life has inspired this book in more ways than one.

And last but not least, to my Glama husband Dr. John F. Demartini. It constantly amazes me how you can look like you've just stepped off the pages of a fashion magazine—even when you have just flown from one side of the planet to the other. You were born with Glama genes—lucky you!

Athena

To my favourite Glama girls—

My mother Shelley, whose fantastic humour, innate stylishness and ability to chop winter kindling while wearing long strings of pearls (and stilettos) has always inspired, and my gorgeous grandmother Ruth, who knows exactly how to be the most adored and stylish queen of her castle. Both of you have the courage of the lioness and true feminine glamour.

To my favourite Glama man and soulmate Giancarlo—your uncanny knack in always looking totally elegant (no matter what you wear!) is absolutely astounding, as is your unconditional love and inspirational pride in me.

Deborah

And from both of us a great big thank you to Fiona Schultz, Robynne, Monica, Roz and all the other Glama girls (and guys) at New Holland. Thanks also to the Australian Society of Plastic Surgeons (ASPS) for invaluable research information, femail.com.au, and the Heart Foundation, for health advice and delicious Glama-friendly recipes.

Visit Athena at www.starwoman.com and Deborah at www.deborahgray.com

'Glamour is like magic; it's an illusion until you make it real.

It's the stuff that dreams are made of.'

Athena and Deborah

GLAMAZON

how to be fabulous, famous and flawless

Athena Starwoman and Deborah Gray

NEW
HOLLAND

First published in Australia in 2003 by
New Holland Publishers (Australia) Pty Ltd
Sydney • Auckland • London • Cape Town

14 Aquatic Drive Frenchs Forest NSW 2086 Australia
218 Lake Road Northcote Auckland New Zealand
86 Edgware Road London W2 2EA United Kingdom
80 McKenzie Street Cape Town 8001 South Africa

10 9 8 7 6 5 4 3 2 1

National Library of Australia Cataloguing-in-Publication Data:

     Gray, Deborah (Deborah Noëlle).
     Glamazon: how to be fabulous, famous and flawless.

     Includes index.
     ISBN 1 74110 105 0.

     1. Beauty, Personal—Miscellanea. 2. Astrology—Miscellanea. 3. Incantations.
     I. Starwoman, Athena. II. Title.

     646.7042

Publishing Manager: Robynne Millward
Senior Editor: Monica Ban
Designer: Karlman Roper
Illustrator: Marc Lynch
Production Manager: Linda Bottari
Printer: Tien Wah Press (Pte) Ltd, Singapore
Cover image: Getty Images
Back cover photo of Athena courtesy of Juli Balla

CONTENTS

INTRODUCTION

If Life is a Stage, Why Not Insist on Better Lighting?

Let's face it—whether we want to or not, we are all playing a role on the stage of life. Why not look your best, slip into some kitten heels, slap on the lip gloss, dress up to the nines, put on an Oscar-winning performance and basically do whatever you possibly can to be fabulous, famous and flawless? So what if you're only a legend in your own lunchtime? It's much more fun to be a glamourpuss with a first-class attitude sashaying through life (even when you feel like a fashion train wreck). And as you learn to pull this kind of glamour off, amazing and mysterious things will start to happen.

Glamour has enormous hidden power. It's like a magic cloak of beauty and charisma, and it's been around since the caveman era, when naughty neanderthal gals first discovered the seductive power of the fur bikini (or was that Raquel Welch in *One Million Years BC*?).

Legend has it that the mystical art of glamour was perfected by the most bewitching women throughout the ages to help attract love and good fortune. And glamour proved so successful that its most powerful secrets were promptly pounced on and jealously impounded by kings and queens. 'After all, it would upset the status quo to have the peasants both revolting and glamorous,' they cried!

No matter how much they tried, however, the aristocrats and the archbishops could not lock all that glamour away from the public forever. Luckily, a small group of royal courtesans—favourites of the king—ran away from the French court with some of the best glam-recipes pinned inside their crotchless panties, including the formula for eau-de-cologne and the first stay-on lipstick (in diva red, of course). Today, everyone from the cleverest politicians to the most famous fashion models and movie stars (and still most of the queens) are so hooked on glamour's power, they pay a fortune to learn it from the experts.

Now you too can learn the keys to a fabulous, glamorous life right here within the pages of this book. True glamour is more than make-up—it's an attitude. And we like to call that attitude, 'Glama'.

So read on and learn how to walk, talk, entertain and handle fame like a true glamour queen—a 'Glamazon'.

Who is a Glamazon?

A Glamazon is a woman who revels in Glama's delicious and seductive alchemy— the sassy, miraculous and magical form of glamour that we too have discovered, and now (selflessly, of course!), reveal to the modern world.

Glamazons are leaders who live in a self-made world of stunning potential and fabulousness. Many Glamazons are famous, but there are plenty of non-famous divas, too. Many are unsung heroes, but all are fabulous and impossibly glamorous to the core. There's always one Glamazon in every family, and if it's not your own wonderful mum or wicked Auntie Nora, then search out your ancestral family album and you'll be sure to find a picture of her there somewhere. She's the stunning one dressed like a movie star, snuggling stylishly up to the hunkiest guy in the place.

Are Glamazons Born that Way?

Not necessarily—but even Eliza Doolittle and Pretty Woman had to have been born with both potential and...the Glama gene. At whatever age, Glama is the essential ingredient for vivacity, charisma and feminine power.

Athena's precocious (three-year-old!) neighbour was born with an acute sense of feminine and theatrical style. She may not yet be able to tie her own shoelaces, but she sure knows what style and colour they have to be and which matching outfit she wants (ballerina tutu at breakfast, mummy's red stilettos for tea).

And Deborah's sassy grandmother has always known about Glama's regenerative powers. At twenty-seven, she was a struggling but stylish divorcee with a mission to remarry well (goal achieved!). Now ninety-three, she is still an absolute Glamazon; she's always one step ahead of everyone, and she instinctively knows what's in and out of fashion.

Real Glamazons are Real Women

Glamazons are not all naturally beautiful, educated, famous or born with a rich daddy; but no matter, they soon find out how to bag, borrow or wrestle what they need from the best of 'em. Even the hottest young chicks around, the Glama babes, don't reach their full glam-potential until they've hit thirty—and then it's still onwards and upwards from there. A real Glamazon:

- Knows how to make an entrance.
- Shall not (and cannot) be ignored.
- Knows that her age is only a number (and a secret one at that).
- Adores men—but only those men worth adoring.
- Knows that her success helps others, her failure helps no-one, and that stockings should never be worn with sandals.
- Knows that modesty is a feminine virtue—and if she can fake that, she's got it made.
- Believes in fulfilling her own destiny, as well as finding the perfect hairdresser.
- Has an iron fist hidden in her long satin gloves.
- Knows a stitch in time saves nine—and a face over thirty-nine.
- Is a total man magnet, but is also prepared to go it alone.
- Knows all about pussy power in this dog-eat-dog world.
- Knows how to housekeep, but prefers to renovate and buy another.
- Does not take 'no' for an answer—except to 'does my bum look big in this?'

- Sets herself the highest standards (and if that doesn't work, goes to plan B).
- Believes in supporting her sisters of the goddess.
- Refuses to hand her power over to others (unless she can delegate or plans to start up another business).
- Is prepared to work long and hard to better herself—and the longer and harder the better.
- Knows that tomorrow is there for the taking, today is the time to act, and next week she can stay in and veg out.
- Is looking forward to ageing—but only gracefully and very very slowly.
- Treats her body like a temple during the working week and like an amusement park on the weekend.
- Never gives in or gives up—especially not her emerald-cut diamond engagement ring.
- Is all woman, but can also think 'just like a man'.
- Has thrown out words from her vocabulary like 'failure' or 'old'; to her there's just birth and one big fabulous life.
- Lets it be known she's ambitious and is not afraid to go for what she wants—she wants it all.

Where Do Glamazons Live?

Glamazons thrive in all kinds of jungles, especially a 'big city' one. That's usually the best spot for them to work and hunt their prey. They also love to hibernate in tropical rainforest retreats, languish by azure blue lagoons, or empower their inner Glama at various ancient temples and fashionable forests around the world.

Glamazons know when to seduce and enjoy, when to rest and retreat, and the best of them are charmed and dangerous. All of them have studied the battle tactics of the (s)experts—those Glamazons who have blazed the diamond-studded trail before them.

So, stretch out on your chaise longue and learn the strategies and keys to Glama power and success.

'Romance is the glamour which turns the dust of everyday life into a golden haze.'

Elinor Glyn

Chapter One

STRATEGIES OF STILETTO POWER

If you don't think of yourself as a Glamazon, nobody else will either. Sure, Snow White had beauty, but the Wicked Queen had the Glama. Which one is your favourite? The old wowsers always make out that the Wicked Queen (the strong, powerful female archetype) is all out evil, and in the end of the story gets what 'she deserved.' But that's just a fairytale written purposely to scare you off and hide the truth from you. In real life, and if the Wicked Queen had read our book, she would not only remain married to the wealthy divorcee, but happily ever after as well. She would be the most glamorous queen of the realm and learn some communication skills, while Snow White would dump Prince Charming and end up doing Weight Watchers commercials.

Love 'em, hate 'em or don't give a toss about 'em, Glama girls will always be that unforgettable breed of women who create their own immortal legends and history and make the world a much more interesting place.

The Glama Link

Can you guess the Glama link between mega celebrities like Kylie, Britney and J.Lo? As musicians they have excellent bone structure, and their biggest talent is being able to jump around for a least three minutes in either hot pants, a bikini or low riders. None of it's very musical, but who really cares? Their biggest talent breakthrough was recognising their own Glama potential. So how about you? You may not want to be a singing superstar or flash your well-toned thighs at the world, but if you crave success in anything, then whatever you have, flaunt it, and even if you don't, pretend you do and flaunt that as well.

Hooray for Glamazons! They claim 'glamour' for themselves and wear it like a magical cape around their shoulders. They dictate their place on Earth, their identity and the power of their own personality. As a result they become trend-setters—role models for hundreds, sometimes millions, of other women. Many women yearn to be a 'go-getter' and to take command of their own life and destiny, but they fail to 'go-get' anything because they just don't believe in themselves. Glamazons who succeed, whether in the public eye or behind the scenes, are definitely women with abundant self-confidence and a strong sense of certainty about what they want—even if they occasionally falter along the way. The cleverest Glama girls learn to know their strengths and weaknesses and accept the fact that there'll be a few unexpected bumps and setbacks along the way. By believing in their own potential they use whatever tools they have at their disposal to get what (or whom) they want with focus, staying power and super-style.

To get a glamorous life, get smart. If you don't have an amazing talent or special skills and can't afford university, don't let that stop you. Life is your best education.

The Key to Success

The key to success as a Glamazon is to keep moving onward and upward without trashing your current life or burning your bridges with the people who support you as you climb up the ladder of success. It gets just as lonely at the top as it does down the bottom—even if the champagne is better.

One thing is certain though, a Glamazon does everything in a more dramatic and exciting style than the rest of the world.

Glamazons of the past took huge chances. These women weren't afraid to buck fashion and find just the right style for them, to pluck their eyebrows into a fine line, to dye their hair (often in outrageous colours), to work-out and tone their body image, to tread the boards in either ballet slippers or stilettos, to study the art of make-up with the diligence of a Picasso or a Rembrandt, to wear fabulous 'look at me' outfits, to make the most of any asset, and to play down any lack of talent or flaws through that illusive power of glamour. Modern-day Glamazons do the same. Think of Cher with her wigs and costumes and Madonna with her ever-changing persona. They use whatever's available and take it to its limit, and somehow, this works for them. Whether you like them or not, you have to admire their success and influence.

If you don't have access to the family Glama tree, don't fret. There are many other women out there to inspire you. Women from the ancient past and present times, who've shown the world how to get sexy, get lucky, get rich, get famous and get laid. Here are some of the most famous examples:

Past:

Cleopatra	Marlene Dietrich
Nefertiti	Gypsy Rose Lee
Coco Chanel	Katharine Hepburn
Mata Hari	Josephine Baker
Jean Harlow	Audrey Hepburn
Mae West	Maria Callas
Lana Turner	Grace Kelly
Vivien Leigh	Marilyn Monroe
Greta Garbo	Jackie Kennedy Onassis

Present:

Donna Karan	Jennifer Lopez
Zsa Zsa Gabor	Elle MacPherson
Brigitte Bardot	Helena Christensen
Goldie Hawn	Nicole Kidman
Shirley Bassey	Anna Kournikova
Madonna	Cameron Diaz
Michelle Pfeiffer	Sharon Stone
Lucy Liu	Iman Bowie
Ivana Trump	Cate Blanchett

Following the Glama path can certainly help make you famous (or infamous). Of course, being a superstar doesn't automatically grant you everlasting happiness—just look at Marilyn Monroe and opera diva Maria Callas. They won the fame and fortune but lost out on love big time. You can learn valuable lessons from the clever Glamazon's moves, as well as from her glaring mistakes.

Every role in life has its pros and cons, but at the very least, those girls who qualified in the Glamazon ranks, did it with panache and unforgettable style. Their lives took them to places and spaces that were exceptional. They met the key players, rulers, movers and shakers of the world, and they often became a key player or mover and shaker in their own right.

Famous or not, Glama girls were, and still are, prepared to apply all their energies and talents into making their lives as fulfilling, rewarding and exciting as possible. Many celebrated Glamazons lived happily ever after, while others soared like a comet and burned out too quickly. But let's face it, feeling gloriously happy one moment and then crashing down in the dumps the next is not exclusive to celebrities. Everyday folks suffer just as many setbacks, broken hearts or misfortunes, except theirs are often kept behind closed doors, without anyone knowing much about it. For your own journey de glamour, it will be up to you to keep a balanced view of life and to try and maintain a positive outlook no matter what.

'Style is knowing
who you are,
what you want to say,
and not giving a damn.'

Gore Vidal

Chapter Two
THE FAME GAME

There are rules that every Glamazon should follow if they're going to make it in the fame game—whether it's in the international arena or as a local sensation.

In all facets of the fashion and entertainment industries, exposure equals income, but when does the fame game become the shame game? Fifteen minutes of shining celebrity can easily be followed by years and years of pathetic 'has-been' status. Unless you're as rich as a Hilton sister with enough society cachet (and cash) to ensure lasting 'shameless celebrity' status, the press can turn its back at a whim, or attack like a pack of wolves.

Think about the sad journey of former reality show inmates. Most of them return to obscurity, while others are desperate to gatecrash the opening of the latest envelope.

From the Diva Diary

Last Tuesday, had a quick but enlightening cappuccino with an acquaintance—one of the top gossip columnists in the land. I ran a few names of would-be celebrities by her, just to check out who's 'in'.

'How about Miss G?' I asked.

'No way!' she spat.

'What about Ms B?'

'Maybe, but she's got more front than a supastore.'

Not to be deterred, I pulled out a couple of magazine clippings and pointed to a very pretty but over-embellished brunette.

'Oh please!' she shrieked with laughter, 'Who the hell is that pathetic chick, and more to the point, who the hell cares?'

Feeling a bit discouraged I flipped over the page to a picture of a tall, buxom blonde hanging off the arm of the latest soap star.

'What about her?'

'Oh yeah, that one I do know, but after a good debut, her fifteen minutes are definitely up.'

'Why's that?' I asked.

'She's been hanging around the gatecrashers ball for too long.'

'Meaning?'

'Meaning you can only be famous for being famous for so long. It's become obvious that this girl's ambition grossly exceeds her talent. By now she should have been able to funnel this publicity into some kind of proper career for herself, but she can't seem to actually do anything or find a job in any part of the industry. She's done nothing but turn up to parties and that's just not enough.'

'So she didn't know how to capitalise on a lucky break and now it's over?'

'Yep. I'll never be printing anything with her in it again.'

'Even if she's still photographed alongside her famous boyfriend?'

'No problem. We just pixelise her out of the shot. Do it all the time.'

'Pixelise?' I asked. 'Didn't the Wicked Queen do that to the Seven Dwarfs?'

'Digital deleting,' she replied. 'The wonders of modern photography.'

I shivered. 'Eeewww. Poor girl. I wonder if she's starting to feel invisible yet?'

'You bet she is,' my well-connected friend said while pointing again to the gossip mag. 'You can already see her confidence dissolving in that photo. See that stiff, fixed look to her grin? She's starting to feel like a phoney. Her star is quickly fading and the photographers will smell that fear a mile away. But she's not the only one. They come and go all the time. It can be a cold, cruel world out there, but there's always the next desperado coming out of the woodwork every social season, grabbing hold of any celebrity in the room and sticking their mug into every photo op.'

'So any words of wisdom to give a budding starlet?' I asked earnestly. 'Can a girl still succeed by using photo opportunities and celebrity social climbing?'

'Oh yes, of course! That's never going to change!'

'Phew! Thank God for that,' I said with great sighs of relief as I moved closer to hear the next pearls of wannabe wisdom.

'Nothing wrong with generating your own publicity and luck,' she continued in a near-whisper. 'Free publicity and invitations to A-list parties are a great way to get your high heels into the door of fame, but publicity is only "free" for a very short time. Eventually you have to pay the piper. Overdo the freebies and you'll get a lifetime exile to photo pixel-land. I mean, honestly, when are these people gonna learn? They'd all be better off staying at home until they've scraped up a smidgen of talent, or even a couple of social skills, rather than wasting our time and ad space.'

As I walked my new best buddy over to her waiting limo, she added, 'Come to think about it, it's a lot more glam and mysterious being an undiscovered talent than a celebrity nobody.'

I pondered over her words and became even more determined to pass on some expert advice to the socially needy.

Handling Media Hounds

To handle publicity like a pro, you must learn the unwritten rules of the fame game, and if breaking into any part of the entertainment or fashion business is on your Glama agenda, luckily for you we've listed the most important rules of all.

Fame Game Rule 1

You must avoid looking like a party-crashing fool, or even worse, a stalker. Being a celebrity nobody is not something a Glamazon should ever aspire to or admit. Why? Because the 'Who's that girl?' or 'The new face on the scene' strategy is only good for a few lucky shots. There's a fine line between those spontaneous photo ops, such as a fortunate stumble into the gallant arms of George Clooney as opposed to elbowing his ageing mother in the ribs to get yourself on camera.

Fame Game Rule 2

'Celebrity professional' should become your keyword. Before you begin your own publicity campaign, get professional and know what you are selling. Every kind of publicity campaign is basically a form of marketing and sales*woman*ship and what you want to achieve out of the PR. No matter what you're selling, you have to know what it is and define it into a clear and precise game plan.

Despite being a cut-throat industry, the members of the media are always looking for a good story to write about, so make sure you have one to give them. Ask yourself these kinds of questions:

- What business do you want to be in?
- What are you selling?
- Are you selling yourself?

If you're promoting yourself, then what part of you are you selling—your body or your mind? Or both? Are you promoting your musical talent or your acting skills? Or are you introducing a new or unusual product into the marketplace? Even if you haven't got a business or a product to sell, what do you have that can be a saleable commodity? What is your best business asset? Is it your looks, your talent, your intelligence, your gift of the gab, a burgeoning modelling career, your own idea for a television or radio program, your latest book, your fashion designs, your own invention (or the rights to someone else's crazy but incredible creation), your art, a new computer game, or your exclusive dog washing business? The key here is to think about what business you're promoting and what's unique about it.

Think of yourself as both the owner and marketing department of your own company. Practice for the real thing by getting some business cards made up and on your computer print out some graphic ideas and names for that business name or company. Any good ideas can be turned into gold with the right publicity, but you need to be able to speak spontaneously about them and to put them into a format that the public and media can understand and help promote for you.

Anything is possible. Recently, the world's first public brothel went up on the stock exchange. Just by the unusual nature of its business (yes Gloria, sex does sell!), and the inspired marketing decision of having one of the most infamous madams in the world on the floor of the Melbourne Stock Exchange during the company's first day of trading, a storm of publicity was generated for its shareholders and, for the time being at least, they've matched it with a storm of profits. So, any outrageous and even some socially 'taboo' businesses can be successfully marketed and accepted by the mainstream media—along with the more conservative branches of business—if approached properly (and if you know how to play the rules of the game).

Trade Secrets

Now, these rules of the fame game are not parted with easily. Many famous and wannabe famous divas regularly pay publicity agents a small fortune for just such insights. The information we are giving you has been honed from years of our own experience in the spotlight and dealing with the media, plus a few pearls of wisdom extracted directly from the source of it all—the executives of the world-wide PR machine.

Publicity agents prefer to keep their trade secrets very close to their chest, for obvious reasons of competition, and don't like to share their mystical secrets with 'outsiders.' Let's face it, most of the gossip columnists and publicity agents are making a very profitable, but quite precarious, living out of doing nothing much more than working with smoke and mirrors and selling illusions of glamour...and bless 'em all. They get paid deservedly well for their amazing 'cold calls' and sleight of hand. Talk about magic and illusionists—the best publicists would give David Copperfield a run for his money! But the other reason they are so successful and respected (or feared) is because each one of them has learned to hone their own natural social skills, networking ability, charm, or sheer bullying power into a damn good business. They've been able to use all their life skills to make the most out of any social occasion. These publicists become an accepted fixture amongst the transitory and fantasy world of parties, charity do's and fashion galas—not an easy thing to do. They've backed up their talent with some kind of education (doesn't matter if it's university or the school of hard knocks), salesmanship and office skills, art, accounting or typing courses, or whatever it takes, and they've made a viable industry out of it. If you look carefully at those who've been around the longest, they are the ones who help to professionally network many different kinds of talented or barely talented people into many different areas of entertainment, sport or fashion, and into the most profitable areas of multimedia business. So they've given something back to the very industry they manipulate and they use it to meet their own ends. This creates a win–win publicity and profit cycle for themselves and others. They've learned to give something back and, voila, they pay the proverbial piper. A lot of them probably started out just like any other wannabe, with one or two chance meetings at a social gathering and, step by step, they turned that charmed evening or lunch into a viable career. You too can use many of these same business principles yourself.

What's your Story?

Even if you don't have a business up and running or you haven't produced a product yet, you'll only be successful if you have at least one good 'story' and have put a future business plan together before you jump tussle-haired first into the publicity spotlight. So when you do manage to get your beautifully made-up mug into a photo opportunity, and that news journalist asks you '...and what do you do?' you have to have a witty and fascinating answer ready for him or her to pass on to their editor. Don't say, 'Ah, well, I'm just here with the roadie/lighting guy/my girlfriend,'—all guaranteed to send you to the rejection pile. This kind of reply (if you dare to), would definitely get a journo's undivided attention:

'I'm shagging the star/lead singer/your boss,' quickly followed by:

'Just joking! Actually, I'm the managing director of (insert business name) television/fashion/records Inc.'

The best case scenario would then be to whip out your groovy business card as they say:

'Oh, really, how fascinating! And just what does your company do?'

And you have the final word by saying:

'Call me tomorrow and I'll give you an exclusive. Got to run, bye!'

Of course, there are those occasions when fate plays its hand before you've crossed all the t's and dotted all your i's. All of a sudden you may be thrust into the limelight simply because your little brother secretly entered you into a magazine competition for that Hollywood A-list party and you won, or your room-mate suddenly makes the *Guinness Book of Records* for growing the biggest indoor tomato in history. Even more bizarre is if Jennifer Aniston gets the flu and you're asked to chaperone Brad to the launch of his latest film!

All such scenarios are goldmines of self-publicising opportunities, and when that kind of thing happens you've got to know how to think on your stilettos, recognise the opportunities, and make something worthwhile out of that brief but shining moment in time...and forget about fifteen minutes. In the 21st century shining moments are never longer than sixty seconds!

Can these tips we're giving you really help to get you toned up and ready for such miracles? Absolutely! And listen up because miracles can and do happen, especially after you've swotted up on the rest of our magical Glama tips! So get ready! Fame and fortune may be just around the corner.

Glamazons Always Have a Plan B

What happens if your grand plan as an A-lister Sister is running a bit off course? Sure it's a cliché, but truly, there's great wisdom behind the saying: 'When one door closes, another one opens.' In fact, that saying should be one of every Glamazon gal's mottos. Naturally, just change the saying around a little to suit you. Mutter to yourself every day: 'I can slam or kick doors open whenever I want!' and you'll soon find that is exactly what happens. Doors will sometimes close in your life unexpectedly and, even for a Glamazon, things won't always run according to plan. But once you get your 'Glama attitude' going full swing, rejection, upsets, delays, divorce, detours or even bankruptcy will be like water off a duck's back. Problems and hardship won't faze you. Ordeals, which are often big deals to lesser gals, will not make one smidgen of difference to your outlook, goals and attitude—or to your plans. All they will do is encourage and inspire you. A little adversity or opposition will help you to grow and expand and to move onto another plan or place.

One major trait you must possess as a clever Glamazon is the ability to summon up, when required, perseverance and composure under duress. Another essential attribute is to recognise when enough is enough and that it's time to make changes and move on. There are key emotional and behavioural signs to watch for when you clearly need to rethink your current situation. Some of the major ones include:

- Growing resentment and bitterness towards others and yourself.
- Sleeplessness.
- Depression or manic hyperactivity.
- Lack of passion and drive.
- A sense of hopelessness.

Learn to watch out for these tell-tale signs and remember the power of adaptability. Then, if a career, purchase, social scene or rocky relationship doesn't come up with the rewards or returns suited to your Glamazon desires, you know you always have Plan B, C, D or even E to fall back on, and you'll be ready to refocus, get over any setbacks and design your life for the better.

Do not overlook the power of change and adaptability—being able to transfer your energy or desires into other ventures—because this trait makes you infallible. A Glamazon with an appreciation of adaptability never knows the meaning of the word failure. What others deem as failure; to you is energy. 'Failure' isn't even in your vocabulary. When something doesn't go according to plan it just means you are ready for the next scheme and the next fabulous adventure.

How Do You Decide On Your Next Plan?

This is a big wide world. There are places to go and people to meet. Sometimes the desirable places or people are right next door to you and sometimes they aren't. But whatever you are doing, make sure you are hanging out in the places you love to be in and with people you love to be around. If you need to move to a new location, investigate where the prosperity and lucky energies can be found (some places are for losers, while others are for winners). Hang around the 'happening' people and you're more likely to find adventure or a romance with someone special than if you go to a place with no connections. If you're ready for a new career or financial investment, you can often check out where the high level action is internationally by studying the stock markets of the world and seeing where prosperity is to be found, or by reading a magazine featuring international properties, showing their value and locations. You probably have some idea of where you want to be next (if your current scene flops) because you'll have your 'what's next' antennae up and your eyes wide open. As a Glamazon, you are constantly looking ahead, checking out where the fun, action and riches are to be found.

Location, location, location doesn't just apply to real estate. It applies to a Glamazon too. Some locations are too hard and some are too easy. Some places will burn you out while others may bore you. The same applies to your exchanges with lovers, jobs, places, family situations, houses, gal pals or travel destinations. What appeals to you today may bore you to death tomorrow. Some mornings you may wake up and know that you need a change of speed, space, place, male companion, friends, currency or even climate, and when that need arises, that's when you immediately shift to Plan B, C, D, E or whatever takes your current fancy. When you operate under the theory that 'there's always Plan B' you will always have an abundance of options in front of you. Consequently there's no such thing as a dead-end relationship, job or situation. Another plan represents another chapter in the fantastic soap opera that is your journey to Glama.

'There's something worse than people talking about you... and that's nobody talking about you.'

Athena and Deborah

Chapter Three

MARTINI LOUNGING

Teetotaller-free zone—no wowsers allowed. Alcohol will duly be served after 6pm. Only cocktail connoisseurs may enter.

Hey, haven't you noticed how everything old is new again, including prohibition? It's back...and so are jazz music, martinis, cigars and cocktail bars. Banned black market speak-easy equals jazz and martinis—all are in vogue. Martini lounging is so cool it's sizzling hot and so is the Glama retro of cocktail teasing.

Your martini lounge style is either roaring twenties Cotton Club or sixties playboy chic. Think Hugh Hefner and James Bond (Connery, of course!), except today, Pussy Galore rules the mansion and she knows how to mix a mean martini to get her chosen boys chilled-out, stirred and shaken. So start frequenting the chicest martini bar in your town, but beware—martinis are powerful so you need to stay aware of your public image. Even the most glamorous women in town can look slack and sleazy after one too many (believe us we've either seen it or been there ourselves). So when out to impress, don't have any more than a couple of drinks, and when in the middle of making a magnificent first impression, never be seen shagging any of those buffed bar staff under the dinner table. It's also a good idea not to go home with that wickedly handsome waiter (well...OK...if you must), but if you sneak home with the rough trade, the key-word is 'secret rendezvous.' Make sure everyone that counts sees you leaving the bar on your own (in your specially hired stretch limo or girl's night out taxi, cos drink driving is for deadbeats in more ways than one).

Martini Musings

Before slipping into your stilettos and sauntering through the door of your favourite cocktail haunt, it may be a good idea to ensure that you are always your most glamorous self by remembering this anti-stumbling affirmation. Recite this drinking ditty before embarking on your cocktail session:

One martini is so lovely—let's sip from our glass
Two martinis are perfect—go to the top of the class
Three martinis spell danger—you'll land on your ass
Four martinis, can't remember—but why is my arm in a cast?

Deborah

Quotes for the Cunning Linguist and Other Witty Ways to Get Laid

Don't you hate it when you're hanging out with the latest rat pack at Harry's Bar and all of a sudden you can't think of a great comeback or home-with-me line? There you are sipping cocktails, dressed to thrill, trying to keep your wits about you, and you need a quick retort, like, now! Well simply slip into the powder room, secretly whip out your Glamazon's guide, and look up this goldmine of witty repartee (with some deep and meaningless affirmations thrown in for good measure!).

Some little snippets you can add to your repertoire include:

- Warning: consumption of alcohol may actually cause pregnancy!
- Smile! It's the second-best thing you can do with your lips.
- One nice thing about egomaniacs—they don't talk about other people.
- A huge load of Viagra was hijacked off the back of a truck a couple of hours ago! The police said they're on the lookout for a gang of hardened criminals.
- If at first you don't succeed, blame it on your parents.
  If at first you do succeed, try not to look astonished.
- Back off, babe! You're standing in my aura.
- I haven't even begun to procrastinate.
- Does the name Pavlov ring a bell?
- We have nothing to fear but fear itself...and those great big furry spiders.
- You don't have to agree with me, but it's quicker.
- I wish I could click my heels together three times and go home. On second thought, I wish I could click my heels together and you'd go home.
- Do I believe in astral travelling? Well I'm having an 'out of alcohol' experience right now!
- I'm trying to understand the psychology of fashion. Did Mrs Freud prefer a slip or a petticoat?
- Promises are like babies: fun to make, but hell to deliver.

- Am I ambivalent? Well, yes and no.
- A hangover is the wrath of grapes.
- Honk if you love peace and quiet.
- If all the world is a stage, where is the audience sitting?
- When blondes have more fun, do they know it?
- Money isn't everything, but it sure keeps the kids in touch.
- All power corrupts. Absolute power is kind of neat though.
- I distinctly remember forgetting that.

Manhattan Mink

If you're in a long term relationship and those bachelor-ette days seem like a distant memory, you can set up your own fabulous play girl pad at home. It's quite easy. Clear out the spare room, stow that sewing machine into the back of the cupboard, search out the retro stores and beg, borrow or steal your granny's old cocktail shakers and padded bar, then recover the matching stools with the glamour of fake chinchilla. Petrossians in Manhattan, the 'sacred' cocktail and caviar haunt of the rich and famous, boasts genuine mink banquette chairs, $500 an ounce beluga caviar and wickedly iced vodkatinis served at the Erté-mirrored bar (divinely lit by Lanvin chandeliers). But if that's not in your neighbourhood then at least you can pay homage to the style.

Put up a row of stick-on mirror tiles to accent your freshly stocked bar, hang a red-beaded curtain over the door frame, vacuum the shag pile or plop down the flokati rug (big enough to wrestle on later), dim the lights, slide the Chet Baker CD into the quadraphonic surround sound system (OK, CD boom box will do), dress in Deco glamour or sixties dolly-bird style, and lead your partner into your seduction cave. Believe us, after just one serve of a Mauve Decade followed by a Lemon Drop Chaser, all the single girl memories and the sex drive will come flooding back to you. Don't forget to put a lock on the door and you'll have created a perfectly fashionable, child- and stress-free haven to enjoy whenever you feel like it.

Gourmet Nibbles to Keep You Standing

Leave those bar nuts for wannabes! What better way to keep company with a cocktail than with the most glamorous nibble food in the world—caviar!

For caviar newbies, Petrossians' expert and ever-so-charming maître d recommends Royal Ossetra Caviar because its taste is so immediate and it has a rich nutty flavour that's accessible and pleasing, even to the novice palate. Beluga's delights are still the ultimate but its sensual flavours can be so subtle that a virgin caviar connoisseur may miss what all the fuss is about.

Cheeky little slices of toast are a sublime way to eat caviar, but for the ultimate Glama taste, try eating it straight from a delicate gold or mother-of-pearl spoon. Yes, this may sound totally decadent but silver spoons can tarnish the flavour. Finally, don't sprinkle superior grades of caviar with lemon or serve them with a chopped egg or onion—that's a big no-no. Save those kinds of garnishes for inferior grades.

A much cheaper but still prized alternative to the top level caviars is salmon roe. Sometimes referred to as red caviar, salmon roe is valued for its larger, firmer beads and juicy sweetness. Combine red caviar with a delectable dollop of crème fraîche (the perfect accompaniment for this succulent roe) and serve with an airy white-flour pancake known as a blini. Blinis look and taste very much like a pikelet. The Russians expressly created them to accompany their best and most beloved caviars.

Besides caviar, try snacking on smoked trout, smoked sturgeon or foie gras (pâté), and of course the glorious old standby—one dozen (or two) chilled natural oysters.

The Perfect Martini Recipes

All Glama girls should know how to stir up the perfect cocktail so they can be the hostess with the mostest. Martini success is only a few moments away. Following are our steps to making the perfect martini and the best martini recipes in town.

The Basics

All it takes to make a marvellous martini are: good quality spirits (both the alcoholic and the mood to party kind), a cocktail shaker, a mixing glass with strainer, a corkscrew, a spirit measure, an ice bucket and ice tongs, cocktail napkins, prepared garnishes, swivel sticks, coasters and a selection of glasses including the classic martini (cocktail) glass and the lowball glass. (Some of the most outrageously glamorous glasses to use are Waterford Marquis glassware and Kosta Boda crystal.) To look the expert cocktail mover and shaker, follow these simple steps when making drinks for your cocktail cohorts:

- Chill the gin (or the vodka), the cocktail shaker and the glasses in the freezer.
- Chill the vermouth in the fridge.
- Always use cracked, not crushed, ice.
- When using the cocktail shaker, the movement should be sharp and fairly assertive, and remember to keep your hands on both parts of the shaker or at least a finger on the cap otherwise you may spill the ingredients. When the shaker is frosted, all the ingredients are nicely blended and cold.
- You may choose to stir rather than shake your drink, but please don't admit that to a true connoisseur—though it's true that stirring is the best way to keep the clarity and potency of the spirits. Use a mixing glass filled with ice and stir carefully to avoid chipping any ice and thus diluting the drink.
- Casually introduce a green olive. Some purists prefer olives free of pimiento (the red stuffing often found lurking inside green olives).
- The ultimate lemon twist is to tie a little knot in the middle of a sliver of lemon peel.

Standard Dry Martini

60ml (2fl oz) gin
7½ml (¼fl oz) dry vermouth
(a dash will do)
1 green olive to garnish

Stir ingredients with cracked ice in a mixing glass, then strain into a chilled martini glass. Garnish with a green olive on a cocktail stick and serve. If you garnish this drink with a cocktail onion, it is called a Gibson.

The proportions and opinions vary greatly on what is truly a dry martini, and the range can take you from somewhat wet to bone dry. Here are some of the more popular proportions and their measures:

- 4 to 1: 60ml (2fl oz) gin and 15ml (½fl oz) vermouth
- 5 to 1: 50ml (1⅔fl oz) gin and 10ml (⅓fl oz) vermouth
- 8 to 1: 60ml (2fl oz) gin and 7½ml (¼fl oz) vermouth
- 12 to 1: 60ml (2fl oz) gin and 5ml (⅙fl oz) vermouth

Beyond that, you should coat the bottom of the shaker with vermouth and throw out any excess before adding the gin.

Medium (or Perfect) Martini

45ml (1½fl oz) gin
15ml (½fl oz) dry vermouth
15ml (½fl oz) sweet vermouth

Stir ingredients in a mixing glass filled with cracked ice, then strain into a chilled martini glass. Traditionally, this martini is served without a garnish.

Traditional Martini

45ml (1½fl oz) gin
22½ml (¾oz) dry vermouth
twist of lemon peel to garnish

Stir ingredients in a mixing glass filled with cubed ice, then strain into a chilled martini glass and serve with a twist of lemon peel.

Sweet Martini

60ml (2fl oz) gin
15ml (½fl oz) sweet vermouth
1 cocktail cherry to garnish

Stir ingredients in a mixing glass filled with cracked ice, then strain into a chilled martini glass. Garnish with the cocktail cherry and serve.

Blenton

45ml (1½fl oz) gin
22½ml (¾fl oz) dry vermouth
dash of Angostura bitters

Stir ingredients in a mixing glass filled with cracked ice, then strain into a chilled martini glass and serve.

Bloodhound

30ml (1fl oz) gin
15ml (½fl oz) dry vermouth
15ml (½fl oz) sweet vermouth
15ml (½fl oz) strawberry liqueur
1 strawberry to garnish

Shake all ingredients with ice in a cocktail shaker then strain into a martini glass. Garnish with the strawberry and serve.

Cordial Martini

37½ml (1¼fl oz) gin
7½ml (¼fl oz) vermouth
7½ml (¼fl oz) cordial Medoc
twist of lemon peel to garnish

Stir ingredients in a mixing glass filled with cracked ice, then strain into a chilled martini glass and serve. Garnish with the twist of lemon peel.

Cosmopolitan Martini

30ml (1fl oz) vodka
15ml (½fl oz) Cointreau
juice of ½ lime
dash of cranberry juice

Pour all ingredients into a cocktail shaker half filled with ice. Shake, strain into a chilled martini glass and serve.

Fino Martini

60ml (2fl oz) gin
15ml (½fl oz) Fino sherry
twist of lemon peel to garnish

In a mixing glass half filled with ice, combine the gin and sherry, stir well and strain into a chilled martini glass. Garnish with the twist of lemon peel and serve. You can substitute the twist of lemon for an olive.

Flying Dutchman

60ml (2fl oz) gin
7½ml (¼fl oz) curaçao

Shake ingredients with ice in a cocktail shaker, pour into a lowball glass and serve.

Gin and It

60ml (2fl oz) gin
30ml (1fl oz) sweet 'Italian' vermouth
1 cocktail cherry to garnish

Stir gin and vermouth in a chilled martini glass with no ice and serve garnished with the cocktail cherry.

Holland Martini

60ml (2fl oz) Dutch Genever gin
15ml (½fl oz) vermouth
twist of lemon peel to garnish

Pour the gin and vermouth into a cocktail shaker half filled with ice. Shake, strain into a chilled martini glass and serve with the twist of lemon peel.

Knickerbocker

60ml (2fl oz) gin
15ml (½fl oz) dry vermouth
7½ml (¼fl oz) sweet vermouth

Pour all ingredients into a cocktail shaker half filled with ice. Shake, strain into a chilled martini glass and serve.

Lemon Drop Chaser

45ml (1½fl oz) citron vodka
dash of triple sec
twist of lemon peel and sugar to garnish

Stir over ice then strain into a chilled martini glass. Some people prefer a piece of sugared lemon peel on the side while others like sugar on the rim of their glass and the lemon as a garnish.

Marsala Martini

22½ml (¾fl oz) gin
22½ml (¾fl oz) vermouth
22½ml (¾fl oz) dry marsala
twist of lemon peel to garnish

Pour all ingredients into a cocktail shaker half filled with ice. Shake, strain into a chilled martini glass and serve with the twist of lemon peel.

The Martinez

60ml (2fl oz) gin
15ml (½fl oz) dry vermouth
2 dashes of Maraschino liqueur
dash of Angostura bitters
2 small ice cubes

Stir ingredients in a mixing glass filled with the ice cubes, then strain into a chilled martini glass and serve.

Martini Royale

90ml (3fl oz) gin
dash of chilled champagne
twist of lemon peel to garnish

Pour gin into a chilled martini glass. Top with champagne and garnish with the twist of lemon.

Mauve Decade

30ml (1fl oz) gin
30ml (1fl oz) vermouth

Stir gin and vermouth in a chilled martini glass and serve.

Paisley Martini

67½ml (2¼fl oz) gin
7½ml (¼fl oz) vermouth
1 teaspoon scotch
twist of lemon peel to garnish

Stir all ingredients over ice cubes in a lowball glass. Add twist of lemon peel and serve.

Pernod Martini

60ml (2fl oz) gin
15ml (½fl oz) vermouth
dash of Pernod
1 olive to garnish

Pour all ingredients into a cocktail shaker half filled with ice. Shake, strain into a chilled martini glass and serve with an olive.

Racquet Club

60ml (2fl oz) gin
15ml (½fl oz) vermouth
2 dashes of orange bitters

Shake with cracked ice, strain into a chilled martini glass and serve.

Vodka Martini

60ml (2fl oz) vodka
15ml (½fl oz) vermouth
1 green olive to garnish

Shake or stir ingredients over ice and serve on the rocks or strain into a chilled martini glass. Garnish with the olive.

Conversion Table
⅛fl oz = 5ml = 1 teaspoon
¼fl oz = 7½ml = ½ tablespoon
⅓fl oz = 10ml = ⅔ tablespoon
½fl oz = 15ml = 1 tablespoon
1fl oz = 30ml = 2 tablespoons
1½fl oz = 45ml = 3 tablespoons
2fl oz = 60ml = 4 tablespoons

'Why don't you slip out of that wet dress and into a dry martini?'

James Bond...Jnr

Chapter Four

MAN SAFARI

Getting a man to meet you, pamper you, marry you, buy you diamonds or...to get lost is all part of a Glamazon's interplay with men. In your journey through life there'll be one or (if your lucky) a few 'keeper' men that you'll want to stay with forever. Then there'll be the ones that you'll just want to get back on the train to Jerksville and stay the hell out of your life. But most will teach you what you definitely do or don't need and then go merrily on their own way to (hopefully!) get a life.

Discover the Tribes of Glama Men

Before you begin your man safari, you need to study the different tribes of 'Glama man' around to help you choose your perfect match. It is crucial to study different nationalities and their cultures. Investigate the differences between Italian, English, Australian, American men etc, and understand how their culture influences them. What are the national interests in the country they come from? What sports are played and supported? What food do they eat? Also listen and learn about how they like their women to be. Knowing all this can give you a head start in attracting your perfect hombre to your midst.

It is also helpful to research the different star signs and personality traits of the men that interest you. For instance, whatever country he hails from, Mr Aries can be dashing, and very, very sexy, but you need to tread lightly so as not to shock him with the reality of a long term commitment. The Taurus Glama guy can be romantic and sensuous, but if you're not careful he can also be a passionate, controlling bully. Gemini boys arefascinating and frustrating and love all the drama of a good challenge, while Master Cancer, is mister contrary but he's so adorable you'll want him to take you home for a lifetime cuddle. And Lord Leo—oh boy!—he's the perfect Romeo to your Juliet, but if you don't keep him sizzling on the boil, he's off like a tomcat. Monseigneur Virgo is mysteriously sexy but can be annoyingly neat and hates chipped toenails and dirty feet, while Mr Libra is the lothario your mother warned you about but is impossible to resist. Signor Scorpio, well what can we say Glama girls? Live dangerously! If you manage to rope a Sagittarius into your cosy barn you'll never be bored, and Mr Capricorn will screw you silly and show you how to be the Director of the Board. Monsieur Aquarius—yikes!—how many heartthrobs can you handle in one night? He's got so many sides to him you'll have to use all your Glama power to get noticed. And Mr Pisces, well fantasies can come true, but unless you know his tricks he'll make out like a wombat (eats shoots and leaves).

You'll be amazed by how much you can learn about men from knowing when and where they were born.

And finally, are you prepared to compromise or walk over cut glass to get what you want? Of course, it's all right to choose to be totally unchanging and independent, but the chances of you being alone or forever single dramatically increase. Nobody is forcing you to hunt down a companion, after all, you may prefer to age gracefully, live alone with your three cats and spend Saturday nights with your gay best friend. But if you do want a partner, you should be absolutely ready and convinced that this is what you want, because once you've walked the Glama road to snaring a man, there's no turning back. If a hot new lover (particularly one you want to stay around) is part of your life plan, then hurl the humble and holy and the casual camouflage out the window, or else you'll be totally invisible to the opposite sex. After all, when addressing the troops before battle, one should always wear their best dress uniform.

Talk the Talk or He'll Walk the Walk

There are certain rules a Glamazon should go by when interacting with men. Some may call it effective communication, but the real Glamazon knows that healthy conversation is also a means of getting what she wants when she wants, with the added bonus of having the guy of her dreams stick around. Glamazons know how to engage in interesting discussions with men, whether they have just been introduced or live together. The Glamazon knows how to express her thoughts and emotions, making any man feel like they are the centre of her universe—a foolproof plan that will stop any man from walking.

But beware girls, we're sorry to report that there are heaps of misguided women out there who have totally lost all connection with their goddess-driven feminine wiles. These gals have taken on the mindset (or otherwise have lost their minds) that it is joyous and fun to act like a complete ball-breaker to all men, whether the poor guy deserves it or not. Most of them would also enjoy being a brickie's labourer, laying down asphalt and making over an old car engine from scratch—yikes! Imagine what these kind of chores would do to any well-maintained Glamazon's manicure! Our advice in these matters is to leave these kinds of activities to the men—chauvinists or not. Most blokes seem to love this kind of heave-ho activity, and who are we to deprive them of their alpha male kind of fun? While there are certain Glamazons who can push a plough and still manage to look great while they're doing it—we know a great female vet who can run down and rope-up a runaway calf while wearing Laura Ashley and gumboots—most Glamazons feel happiest getting their exercise in a fitness class with other Glama gals, or on their treadmill at home. Glamazons don't mind getting sweaty, as long as it's for a good cause—their own health and beauty.

There are lots of Glamazons who enjoy polishing their own diamonds, making reservations, checking that their elaborate pot plants are well-watered and shopping for cars and other fine machinery—they just don't want to have to maintain everything themselves, and generally do the nuts and bolts kind of things. Sure a Glamazon can change a light bulb and fix a fuse, and if she puts her mind to it, she has no problem programming the new DVD or video mobile phone either (because, let's face it, they are useful). But anyone with a brain knows that a woman who is seriously smart from the neck up (with a bod maintained for the joys of sin), can receive unlimited rewards allocating her precious time into what she has a real passion (and makes a good salary) doing.

There are also women who really enjoy being total bitches to men (and men who are mesmerised by rotten-to-the-core minxes) and more power to 'em. Different strokes to different folks, we say. Then there are women who become man haters, for whatever right or wrong reason, and they become bitter and twisted at an early age and feel constantly weighed down in life with huge chips on their shoulders—hopefully they'll search out some well-needed therapy to enable them to move on and let go of those past hurts and disasters. Whether they choose to be single or in a relationship, it's essential that they learn how to break through those kinds of barriers in order to accept love again. Let's face it, all women—including Glamazons, ball-breakers and ultra feminists alike—are forged from the same stuff of the goddess...the Goddess Venus (or Aphrodite as she is known in other circles).

It's just that an ultra feminist might like to fend for herself entirely, while a strong-minded Glamazon cherishes her independence but still loves to be treated like a female, as well as a sensitive, creative and sexy woman. The fact is a Glamazon just doesn't want to fire bullets from the frontline, or chop the wood, or fix the broken machinery, or dig ditches (unless there is no other alternative or no man around to do it). The feminist movement did a whole lot of good for women and goddess power in general. It helped women get the respect they deserve in the home and workplace. There's really nothing women can't do now—they can have it all and the right guy (or girl) by their side. Women can follow any path they choose. Large sections of the women's movement are also coming around and realising that men aren't all bad—they're really quite useful occasionally!

But seriously, many women around the world are nostalgic for the romance of a beautiful old-fashioned courtship, and are remembering how to appreciate a man opening the car door for them (and saying thank you when being offered his seat or given a compliment). A Glamazon will always allow the right man to treat her like a princess, to buy her gifts for no reason at all, to send her flowers and to spoil her rotten when she needs some extra TLC. So thank you feminists because it took that kind of 'balls' and a revolutionary spirit to make the big changes and to wake up the chauvinistic misogynists of this world. How fantastic it is to now live in a world where women have earned the respect they deserve and still have the right to dress up to the nines and play sexy games like 'Guys and Glamazons.' So when indulging in this pastime, follow these sure-fire techniques to keeping any man by your side:

- Be comfortable in talking about yourself and your achievements when you are asked about them. Men will enjoy learning about this unique side of you. Just make sure you take a breath occasionally and let him impress you as well.
- Listen to what subjects he discusses with his friends and find out what his hobbies and interests are. Talk about things that men enjoy discussing in general, such as sports, cars, current affairs, music or the arts. You'll show how you can be just as fun as his buddies are, and how in tune you are with what he likes.
- If you find a man insulting or rude, express your distaste openly. Glamazons never accept this sort of behaviour.

- Never permit a man to interrupt you. If he does, tell him not to. This will really get his attention!
- The opposite of that coin is never interrupt a man's flow of conversation at a social occasion. He'll lose his cool totally—it's something to do with the way his brain is wired. Women can juggle three conversations at a time, but men cannot (and they hate to fail at anything!).
- Never curse or use foul language—it really turns men off (except when you're admiring the size of his johnson).
- Give him time and let a man chase you, but if that doesn't get you anywhere, don't be afraid to ask a man out—the shy ones often appreciate that you do!
- Always let a man know when you are angry. They're not mind readers and like to know how you feel. But if he flirts too much, wait until you get home before you slap his face.
- Never bring up past problems or old relationships with a man you have just met. You'll look like you have a chip on your shoulder or are still healing from a bad break-up and he'll walk away as fast as you can say, 'I'll get some therapy!'
- Don't drop your head down when talking and act like a victim. Be assertive and make eye contact when talking to a man. Not only will he know you are confident, but you'll mesmerise him with the colour and sparkle of your eyes!
- Keep your voice pitch low if you want to show that you're a strong woman and under control. But if you want him to take you to bed straightaway, giggle at his jokes like a little girl.

Every Glamazon should remember that even though you may be desperate for a date, you should never ever show it. The desperado look is dullsville—go for 'hot and hungry' instead. But golddiggers beware; there is nothing wrong with digging for gold, just get ready to wallow in the mud for many years before hitting pay dirt! You may need to know how to get hooked on Valium and pretend you love your rich old husband for at least ten years before hitting the jackpot—can't be done unless you're an absolute ice queen.

Besides, nowadays there's no need to shack up with someone you aren't crazy about anyway. There are plenty of youngish, obscenely successful divorcees or ex-playboys around—go for the independently wealthy ones of course! Don't believe us? How about the Glamazon standby…our secret stash of sex gods. Dirty rotten scoundrels can be very sexy…and eligible. Think of ageing playboys, who can be great in bed and look great on your arm at movie premieres (but only after they've inherited their sugar-mammas fortune). When ex-Don Juans finally wake up to the joys of true love, they are too tired and knowing to run off with a younger woman and they have a great sense of humour (they had to, to survive their previous careers). The only exception to the retired playboy rule is ageing rock stars—avoid them like the plague. They never get tired of running after younger women (eternally hyper from either cocaine or their Peter Pan complex), and they ain't never gonna know when to stop—just ask Jerry Hall.

Another tip for the financially-minded Glamazon is to wait until you see the glint of their credit cards (or the green in their wallets). If you have to pay on the first date, expect to do the same for the rest of the relationship. There's also the Girl Scouts' motto: 'Be prepared'. Why not earn your own pot of gold and become independently wealthy instead?

Goldystocks and the Wee Toad— a Glama Fairytale

Once upon a time in a land far, far away, while contemplating her recent stock options and property investments, a glamorous, independent princess called Goldystocks, chanced upon a frog as she sat beside her freshwater spring, which bubbled through the rolling hills near her fabulous newly decorated castle.

Suddenly, the frog leapt upon Goldy's lap and said, 'Gorgeous lady, I was once a very well-connected young prince until a terrible troll cast a spell upon me. However, just one kiss from your tender lips and I will be instantly turned back into the broke but hunky young aristocrat that I really am. Then my sweetness,

I will let you marry me for my A-list title and I'll move into your gorgeous new palace with my old mum, where you can cook for me and my darling mama, clean my clothes, bear me four children, sign over half your money, and of course feel absolutely contented and forever grateful doing so.'

Later that night, as Princess Goldystocks dined delicately on an exquisite feast of poached frog's legs in lime and dill sauce, she took another sip of her private vintage chardonnay and chuckled to herself, 'In your friggin' dreams, mate.'

Men with Potential

Historically, Glamazons have a complicated and multi-layered relationship with men and money. Deborah's Glama grandmama reckons that it's just as easy to fall in love with a rich man as it is a poor one. And one of Athena's Glama girl-friends swears that even though her adoring (and adored) husband may be short and balding, he sure looks tall, dark and handsome when he stands on his wallet. May sound a tad materialistic to some, yet we know these women work hard and long hours most of their lives, whether in their own careers or business partnerships with their husbands, and they are dedicated mothers. They are also loyal to the core, big-hearted and kind to their friends and family—all the elements of heart and spirit any man could wish for in a great girlfriend or wife. Before meeting our soulmates, both of us spent years in all kinds of relationship dynamics, both the financial and the spiritual kind. We always worked hard in our jobs and usually had no problem paying our own way. Consequently, we had no qualms about sharing the costs in a relationship; taking a guy out to dinner occasionally or even going so far as to finance a boyfriend's career change or wacky invention. Needless to say, some of this was greatly appreciated and enhanced the relationship, but quite a lot of it was like pouring love (and money) into a bottomless pit. But the beauty of having a Glama attitude is that we are all strong and independent survivors and, especially in matters of love, Glamazons learn to brush off the cobwebs, let go of the losers and go on to shine through another day. There's a wonderful golden-years-of-Hollywood movie called *The Unsinkable Molly Brown* that sums up the Glamazon attitude best. In the film, Molly Brown, played by the irrepressible Debbie Reynolds, is a fireball of determination, witty humour, ambition, guts and man magnetism. But to cap it all off, she also has the uncanny ability to always fall in love with men of great potential—even when the guy starts off as poor as a church mouse. Once he pairs up with Molly, with her endless drive and luck-producing attitude, her guy with potential miraculously turns into a man of wealth and substance. It's a great old flick and based on a true story.

Of course, if you have the patience and dedication, you could hone your own magical instincts and psychic skills as well (see Chapters Eleven and Twelve), to help you know when to spot a guy who's a solid worker and knows what he wants—a sure-fire way to success.

Whether you want to land a creative but starving genius, or a fabulous guy on the ladder to success, or a fella who's already financially secure, walk right away from any man who yells at waiters and is rude to service staff. Even if he's filthy rich with movie star looks, the laws of the Glama universe say that his kind of wealth is on shaky ground and will eventually be taken away from him. Besides, he'll never let you enjoy your share and he doesn't have any idea how to let his guard down and treat you like the goddess you are.

A good solid catch—a real Glama man—is generous with his heart, as well as his bank balance. If he's dirt poor but makes you feel a million dollars, then who gives a damn? With your amazing Glamazon attitude, the right dose of love, a dash of self-made luck, working together as a team, the world is your enchanted oyster.

A Final Word...on Younger Men

Madonna has one, Cher's had quite a few, Joan Collins has taken it to a new high and most of the greatest girls we know would agree—there's nothing like the adoration of a young stud to leave you simply breathless. A dose of young love is a Glamazon's favourite health tonic, especially when one has been stressed out by a messy divorce. But remember! Boy toys are for medicinal purposes only (nowadays a toy boy is fifteen or more years younger than you—anyone older is totally fair game). Younger men should be taken twice a day until you've finished the entire course of treatment. Once this therapy is over, quit immediately. To avoid youthful overdoses, remember the three Rs—Rejuvenate, Revive and Relocate.

'If you want him
to adorn you
in pearls,
learn how to
polish his jewels.'

Athena and Deborah

Chapter Five

FASHIONISTA SECRETS

Many wise fashion gurus have decreed: 'The best way to progress from rags to riches is to get out of rags' and most true Glamazons would agree with them! While being adorned with a Glama attitude is the ultimate rocket fuel to success, it helps when this confident attitude is gift wrapped in the right clothes and presented with the best personal style. While a fashionista sense of style is certainly not sufficient to transform someone into a Glamazon, it can be a huge step to becoming one. After all, on all levels of this visually-oriented social world, clothes do mean a lot. Think of the hours of shopping and deliberation any career girl, domestic goddess, yummy mummy or sporty sensation invests in organising and deciding, 'Yikes! What will I wear?'

But how on earth can you look like a diva unless you can afford to shop like one? Sure, uber-wealthy babes and A-list celebrities can afford their own fashion stylist and personal shopper, but still, loads of them get it sooo wrong! If you ever need a laugh, just flip through a few of the social pages and gossip mags and have a look at what those gals are wearing on the red carpet—it will make your day. You'll be amazed to see that it cost someone an absolute fortune to look exactly like a blue chicken or a bag lady. Obviously all the money in the world can't buy a true sense of style, and perhaps it's the Zone Diet that's removing all their taste as well as their fat?

How to Shop Like a Diva

Everyone makes a fashion blunder occasionally, but even if you're on a strict budget, you can still dress stylishly and even spend a divine couple of hours being fussed over at the ritziest store in town. Believe it or not, once every season, you can actually walk out of that lavish store with a fabulous new designer outfit and their signature shopping bag swinging from your arm. Impossible you say? We've both spent quite a few years living in one of the biggest fashion capitals of the world, as well as one of the most expensive—New York City. Believe us when we say that to make it in that competitive town you need to dress to impress for just about every business meeting and social occasion. And it wasn't always easy doing that, especially in the first year or so of arriving, while trying to find a safe, comfortable apartment and a well-paying job, not to mention having to live on personal savings while waiting for green cards and working visas to come through. But there are a lot of clever ways to look stylish and up to date anywhere in the world, even on a not-so-glamorous budget. Here's how to do it:

- Never impulse buy.
- Every $20 you don't spend on that incredibly cheap but trashy bargain (that clogs up your overstuffed wardrobe and never fits you right anyway) is $20 lost towards some designer outfit or a brilliantly made piece of clothing that you will always look great in.
- Put that same $20 in a special piggy bank every time you successfully fight the urge. Hold that impulse ten times (that'll probably take the average shopaholic no more than a week!) and, voila, suddenly you can afford the $200 Emporio Armani belt you've been drooling over.
- Put that same $20 in a piggy bank twenty times and you can proudly walk into the Gaultier summer sales and pick up a hand-painted t-shirt or a gorgeous pair of collector jeans that fit you like a glove.
- Be classically styled rather than a slave to style. Avoid grabbing the latest fad off the rack before thinking it through. Will it really add to your personal look and wardrobe?

Love slave sometimes, but fashion victim? Never! Do your flower-embossed mules clash with your ocelot overcoat (faux, of course)? Are you overdosing on retail therapy? In danger of mainlining on Missoni or losing your house with label lunacy? If you're starting to hide your maxed-out credit cards under the cat, then perhaps it's your fashion sense that should be put into protective custody. Here's how not to overdose on fashion trends:

- Regularly check to see whether you're overspending on fashions that fade away after only one season.
- Every once in a fashion file, look at how many of this year's must-haves you've bought. If you've purchased more than a half a dozen of these kind of trendy fads then, yes, you are seriously heading for fashion victimhood. There is also a risk of turning up to a movie premiere or a gallery opening wearing the same outfit as another Glamazon if you overload on clothes from the one season.
- In the middle of every season, before you fall for any more 'you can't live without it' buys, do a stocktake of your own wardrobe. As you tick off each item of clothing, think about whether you really look good in it, or whether, deep down, you know that you look like an idiot or even worse—a fat idiot.
- Seriously now, do those fanny-skimming army cargo pants with the huge thigh-fattening pockets really suit you? Go and take a peep in a two-way mirror and have a good look at yourself from the back. Mmmm, not really?
- Do you do wholesale? The richest Glamazons in town rarely pay full retail for designer wear. They are always looking out for a bargain (how do you think they got so rich!), and although very few will admit it, most smug fashion mavens and magazine editors never pay full retail either. These fashion doyens either get freebies or big discounts off haute couture collections. Naturally, top fashion editors have the advantage of being able to give extra advertising space, or grant certain designers a 'free' plug in their columns.

One trick you can emulate from these clever fashion vixens is to get on all your favourite designers' mailing lists. It really is easy to do. Simply walk confidently into their store or go to their website and ask to be put on their list so you'll always know when it's sale time. Many stores start their sales in the middle of the season—not at the end. You'll be dressed in this year's look and you'll own a well cut, classic design that will last you more than one season. Find out where the big designer outlet stores are in your area. These are usually large warehouses filled with seconds, overstock or so-called 'last season' designer wear at twenty per cent to as much as seventy per cent off recommended retail prices. You have to be prepared to trawl through a lot of racks filled with no-go's, but it is totally worth it when you can pick up such fantastic bargains on many top collections.

'Designer' doesn't have to be the likes of Versace or Prada either. There are many new, up-and-coming designers out there who haven't yet hit the stratospheric price range. Before hitting the big time, Collette Dinnigan used to flog her stunning little slip dresses next to Paddington markets—there's still undiscovered genius out there for $100 or less! You can buy the top fashion magazines and the more alternative rag-trade mags and search the pages for articles on hot new designers who make the kind of clothes you look and feel great in and then find their nearest stockist. They're usually half (or even less) of the price charged by the older, more established designers. The main criteria here is to make sure their clothing flatters your figure, the design has a good cut and finish (no frayed hems or frayed button holes, no matter how much they tell you 'it's the latest style'), and that they use top-quality material.

Apart from checking the labels, don't be afraid to make like a fashionista and get a good thumb and finger feel for fabric and the type of lining used, if any. You can't go wrong with good wool blends, pure cottons and top-quality jerseys and linens. It's all too easy to get trapped into buying that hot new designer jacket, but after a couple of dry-cleans, you may find that the cheap mix of material they've used gets 'iron shine' or their adorable hand-knitted sweater starts to bobble and pill and stretch out of shape. Yuck! If that happens, take it back immediately for a possible refund or put it in the Salvo bin.

Mix and Match

If you can't afford a complete designer outfit, don't worry. Often, wearing the coat, shirt and matching pant together looks too overdone anyway. Invest in just one stunning 'this season' shirt or jacket and wear it with a less expensive but classically cut pant, skirt or best fitting jeans you have. Another Glama trick—a valuable style secret of legendary divas such as Audrey Hepburn and Marilyn Monroe—is to buy several colours of the same great piece of hard-to-find-but-classic Glama wear. If you discover the perfect pant, sexy but wearable shoes, or the ultimate skirt or sweater, purchase the same item in your favourite hues. One of the biggest pains when rummaging through your wardrobe, or when looking for something new to buy, is finding something that fits you exactly right and flatters you perfectly. Every body has a perfectly cut style of clothing that will always look good on that shape and height—the trick is finding it. If you discover such a well-fitting item, then that is the time to invest in your wardrobe future—you won't be sorry. If you can't afford to splurge on everything at once, lay-by at least one more of your flattering item and must-have colour and fit.

Jewellery Gems

If you can't afford good, stylish jewellery, don't wear any at all. It's much better to reveal the sensuousness of a bare neck, or be adorned with a simple fine-gold necklace along with some delicate nine-carat gold earrings, than jangling around like a sideshow gypsy with heavy and horrendous copies of Chanel and Bulgari. Clever and inexpensive costume jewellery, whether it's oversized or delicate, can look great with the right outfit, especially jewellery with an individual 'rich hippy' style or a new, cutting edge look. But never ever wear logo emblazoned designer copies—you may as well have, 'I've got no style of my own and I can't afford to buy any' stamped on your forehead. A good tip with the cheaper brands of costume jewellery is to steer clear of fake gold—it usually rubs off quickly into the dirty looking steel colour that's underneath. When faking it, stick to plated silver or pewter shades of metal. And if you want to avoid black tarnish marks appearing on your nibble-ready earlobes (never a good look), always remove costume jewellery when you have a shower or take a swim in Count Roberto's pool (or that midnight skinny dip at Copacabana Beach).

Bag it Betty

The same 'classic' rule goes for handbags and belts as well. If you can't afford the real thing, walk straight past those street market Vuittons and Chanels and instead, every year or two, depending on how well you look after them, buy yourself a good quality, soft leather, black, non-logo encrusted shoulder bag or clutch and a quality black leather belt. If you can afford it, buy another set in navy or dark brown—whatever shade coordinates best with the majority of the items in your wardrobe.

Find the right bag and belt and they will be just about all you need to accessorise daywear and dressy-but-casual outfits for just-after-sunset soirees. The exception is during sunny summer and late spring days, when you can substitute the leather bag with a fun straw carry-all in this summer's 'in' colour or a stylish natural canvas tote for warm spring barbecues. For a summer belt, sling a colourful silk tie through the belt loops of your spotless white denim skirt or tie a thrift shop Pucci scarf to the strap of your bag to blend with the colour of your outfit. Whatever you do, remember that carrying off Glama style on a tight budget means choosing 'simple' but well-cut or quality items for your staple wardrobe and accessories.

Shoes Glorious Shoes

Sale or full price? Depends on what turns you on the most. Does the thought of getting shoes on sale hit your G-spot or must you snap up those Manolo mules even before they arrive at the store? Grasshopper, those are some of the harder questions in life. Look within because only you can answer them.

Yes, it's really hard work to avoid salivating over the latest release of your favourite designer shoes, no matter how outrageously expensive they are. And, we have to agree, wearing a fabulous new pair of shoes for the first time is like illicit sex. If you have to do it, then goddamn it, go ahead and do it! Just like all sexy fetishes, make sure you're protected (don't sink your life savings or use your room-mate's credit card doing it), and think twice if you're going to ruin all the sublime pleasure with a lingering case of the guilts.

The Epitome of Class— Understated Quality

The more understated and elegantly simple the bag or belt, the less people will notice how often you wear it. The more simple and classic the little black dress, the more you can get away with redressing it with lots of different jackets, pumps and jewellery. Even if people do figure out your budget tricks, the real style queens and Glama men among you will secretly admire just how clever and inherently classy you are. The hordes of fashionistas around the world know that designer wear can be bought, but natural class cannot.

Don't worry if you haven't found your 'inner class' and style yet. While it's true that a wardrobe full of expensive clothes can only be attained by the very rich, real lasting style can eventually be achieved by anyone who cares enough to look, listen and learn.

The Glama approach to understated quality is to have timeless coordinates in your wardrobe to mix and match with one another or with this season's trends. The trick is to buy well-made, classic clothes with sleek lines and a good cut that will last for years. Below are the basic but eternal Glama classics that you can mix and match endlessly and embellish with splashes of colours, jewellery and accessories that would see you dressed to the nines across the seasons in any country in the world:

- Two sleeveless little black dresses—both knee length; one sexy with a plunging neckline for the evening and the other with a rounded neckline for during the day.
- One long, strapless or spaghetti-strapped dress for more formal evenings (in your most flattering shade of red).

- Well-cut pant suit in either black or grey.
- Two or more white cotton, collared shirts.
- Two fabulously fitting white tees.
- Two fine wool or cashmere cardigans—one in black and the other in camel.
- Two slim-fitting black skirts—one mid calf length with a side split and the other a classic knee length.
- One pair of slimline black stretch pant or capris.
- Two cotton mix turtlenecks—one a dark shade and the other white.
- Two pairs of black shoes—one a sexy strappy high heel and the other a low heel court shoe.
- One pair of casual loafers or ballet slipper flats in either black or tan.
- One pair of stilettos or kitten heel pumps in your favourite diva red.
- Two pairs of well-cut denim jeans—one blue and the other white.
- One white or blue denim jacket.
- An understated black leather jacket (bomber style is OK, but leave the bikie look alone!).
- Black, knee-high leather boots, medium heel.
- Classic trench coat either knee or mid calf length in camel or fawn.
- Good winter overcoat either mid calf or ankle length in black or camel.
- Extra large fine wool or pashmina wrap in black.
- Black opaque pantyhose.
- Super sheer black stockings attached to a sexy garter belt.
- One piece swimming costume either strapless or halter neck in classic black, navy and white or leopard print.
- One gold or silver/pewter satin camisole top.
- One black and one tan handbag.
- One black and one tan leather belt.
- Jackie O style sunglasses.
- One string of pearls.
- One leopard print silk or fine cotton scarf.
- One red cotton kerchief.
- An Audrey Hepburn style sun hat.

Fashion Advice from the Designers Themselves

Shhhh! Just between you and us, the designer trick to Glama is to never go cheap on shoes, a belt, a coat or a bag. The Caten twins, the sizzling hot designers from dsquared[2] (they designed Madonna's cowboy gear for her 'Don't Tell Me' video and 'Drowned' tour) might have high-flying clients who can buy anything their stunning little hearts desire, but according to our friends in fashion, those boys also know how to cleverly mix and match non-designer and cheaper items around more high quality coats and other essential accessories.

We are also privy to the fact that even though those gals working at the hippest new fashion mag may promote all the top designers, they'd be the last ones to recommend spending your life savings on new Gucci sandals, leaving no cash for a decent pedicure. The latest on the Glama grapevine is that A-list designers like Miuccia Prada think women become less and less sexier the more flesh they expose. Apparently Madame Prada is totally bored with certain gals of fashion who insist on flashing their stomachs morning, noon and night.

Colour Connection

Every Glamazon discovers what colour suits her the best by examining her skin tone. She also keeps in mind that changing her hair colour can affect her skin tone too. All you have to do is stand in front of a mirror in a room with good daylight and look at your skin tone and the colour of your eyes. Do you have yellow or pink tones in your skin? Do you look tired and drained? Are your eyes dull or vibrant?

The colours that a Glamazon wears must always look perfect next to her face without make-up or accessories. The right colours should enhance what already looks good, so work out what colours suit you best and buy clothes according to this. Mid-tones, clean and bright colours, in general, tend to give the eyes and skin life. Designers usually select a range of colours in their season collections, so there should always be a colour that works for you. Most people can wear a wide range of colours anyway, but it's the intensity of the colour that makes it either right or wrong for you.

As a rule, your wardrobe should consist of sixty per cent colour and forty per cent basic (black, navy, white, brown, stone and grey coordinates). If your wardrobe consists of a mixture of light, dark, bright and pale colour; very little will coordinate. To make your clothes mix and match, you need to work with the same level of intensity in the colours. You will also need to buy clothes that coordinate with at least two to three items already in your wardrobe. Here is a flawless guide to having a gorgeous Glamazon wardrobe:

- If you have blonde, light brown or grey hair; blue, grey, light green or light brown eyes; and clear, ivory skin, you should wear soft colours in light tones. Silver, light gold jewellery works best, as do black, brown and navy accessories.
- If you have medium to dark brown or black hair; grey, green or brown eyes; pale or rosy skin tones or a natural tan, you should wear medium colours that are cool and crisp. Silver or gold jewellery suits you best as do brown, black, tan and navy accessories.
- If you have red, chestnut, auburn or rich black hair; bright blue, green, or hazel eyes; a natural golden tan, freckles, olive skin or dark skin, then deep, rich colours as well as earthy tones work best for you. But for the ultimate Glama look, drape yourself in gold jewellery and wear tan, brown, navy and black accessories.

'Wrap yourself
in glamour...be
the best-dressed
girl in town.'

Athena and Deborah

Chapter Six

VANITY CAN SAVE YOUR LIFE

Amanda the ageing model was contemplating suicide. As she tearily pictured the morning paper's headlines: 'AGE-ING MODEL FOUND IN THE NUDE!', immediately the words, 'Thank God I've lost five kilos' jumped into her mind. Instead of popping sleeping pills, she immediately picked up her phone and called her personal trainer.

Money can't buy you love. Nonsense! If you can't find love then go ahead and buy some by investing in self-love. Spend your money on the gym, personal trainers or beauty parlours—whatever it takes to look and feel fresh, gorgeous and sex-a-licious. Sure that piece of real estate may be a great investment, but don't forget to finance your own temple of self-worship—your body. It'll be the best money you'll ever spend.

If excess weight or body image is your problem then stop whingeing about being lonely, unloved and unattractive, put down that Big Mac and milkshake, go wash your greasy hair and do something about your appearance immediately! If those beginner yoga classes haven't helped, then stop contemplating your navel and move that BFA (big fat ass) onto the treadmill. Here's your new Glama mantra: 'I deserve the body of a sex-goddess.' If the treadmill's too boring for you, then there's always the ultimate Diva work-out.

Stiletto Stretch

There are two dinner date versions of this exercise—the Tablecloth Teaser and the *Nine and a Half Weeks* Rendition. The Tablecloth Teaser is where you skip dessert, kick off your high heels and delicately stretch out your legs, point your toes and play footsies with your lover under the dinner table. The *Nine and a Half Weeks* Rendition is usually performed after arriving back at the playboy/girl pad with accompanying music and consists of leaning against a doorway in silhouette and performing various leggy poses in stilettos, with or without clothes.

Cocktail Flex

These are two excellent work-outs, easily performed while perched on a bar stool. The first is the Pelvic Pull. Contract your pelvic muscles up, hold them for ten seconds and then release. Do this ten times throughout the night. The second is the Tummy and Butt Tuck. Sit up straight on the chair or bar stool, flex your butt muscles and hold in your stomach muscles for ten to fifteen seconds and release. Repeat the action throughout the evening.

Purse Pilates

Who needs a dumb-bell when your handbag will do just as well? Fill your clutch purse with your cosmetics, mobile phone, money etc (just wearing a heavy shoulder bag all night is not recommended as it may strain your neck and shoulders). In private moments, grab your purse and perform various side arm raises and bicep curls.

Every Glamazon should worship her body as a house of health and vitality. In this age of diet fads and gimmicks, the Glamazon knows how to have a healthy approach to keeping fit and loving her body as it is. She knows how to maintain a nutritious eating plan and exercise program to suit her lifestyle and she accepts her gorgeous shape, whether it's lean, buxom, short or tall. Both of us are constantly being asked by women to create some sort of magic to zap them into an instant supermodel body! Don't we wish it was that easy! 'Kaa-zing! You're now Cindy MacPherson Schiffer and you're the most famous supermodel in the world!' We'll get back to you on that later—when we've come up with just the right formula. Hey, who knows?

Naturally, focusing on healthy eating and a moderate exercise regime is essential to keeping fit, and we highly recommend it, but be forewarned—there is a big difference between a healthy exercise and eating plan and fanatical 'dieting'. In this body-conscious age, it's so easy to get caught up in the yo-yo starvation/binge trap. To successfully maintain a good body image and come out of the fanatical dieting and overexercising cycle depends a lot on your own willpower and the ability to wake up to the dangers of being so obsessive about your weight. If there are constant problems, then seek counselling to discover the root of your bad body image. But we can also offer you some of our own insights into the world of glamour and the body beautiful—for instance, what's going on with those 'perfect model bodies' that confront us all day every day on the magazine stands. After long careers in both fashion modelling and the entertainment world, both of us know many of the magical tricks and hidden secrets of the business of beauty. During Deborah's fashion modelling days, she became so obsessed with the right 'look' that she managed to completely reshape her curvy body into a straight up and down stick figure. Pretty impressive, huh! Well, she thought so at the time. Here is what she has to say about her experience:

Like a lot of young girls, I loved flipping through the glossy pages of magazines like Vogue, Cosmo *and* Dolly *and I would spend countless hours daydreaming about the exciting life of a fashion model, right up until my daydream came true. I won a Teen Model of the Year competition when I was fifteen and thus began a career in fashion modelling. I was signed with two of the best agencies in Australia—Vivien's Management and, later, Chadwick's Models. Virtually overnight, I started being booked for some great assignments (despite a few too many late night parties), and being seen in all my favourite fashion magazines, as well as appearing on the catwalks and in countless television commercials for anything from chocolate bars to fast cars. Right through my teens and into my early twenties, I was working with the best photographers, magazines and advertising agencies in the business. And I loved the illusion and the glamour of all of it...at least, for a while. Somehow I'd been given a chance to move up to the 'big city' and live out my greatest fantasy, but after a while, the fantasy got a bit tarnished. I had started modelling with just the usual teenage insecurities and normal kind of body angst, but pretty soon my little bit of teenage body angst blew up into a huge, horrible complex. Not only did I see all those skinny beautiful girls in the magazines, but I actually had to work every day with them and stand alongside all these thin and emaciated young bodies the fashion world seems to admire so much. All of us girls were in competition with each other in auditions, castings for assignments, and on the catwalk. The constant comparing led to my unreal perception of a normal female body.*

I've always enjoyed keeping fit by swimming and dancing and never worried too much about my weight before, but I started seeing my naturally curvy body as something to be despised. I had a distorted view of my own body and believed that it was holding me back in my career. Yes, I was busy, but if I could get rid of my boobs and hips, then I would be even busier. I decided to begin a strict diet and exercise regime to make sure I was accepted and the 'perfect model shape.'

Naturally, overdieting and spending days on end at the gym is ridiculously bad for you. At one point, I was so under normal body fat levels that my period completely stopped for almost eighteen months. But guess what? My new, totally unhealthy and starving 'waif' shape was so totally in fashion, all my modelling clients thought I looked 'fabulous darling!' The modelling assignments and magazine covers flooded in. And lo and behold, the closer I got to looking like a stick insect, the more successful a model I became. Before long, I was caught on this stupid merry-go-round. I wasn't the only one. With very few exceptions, most of the girls involved in fashion modelling were either starving themselves or overexercising just to maintain their so-called 'enviable and highly fashionable' bodies. And it's hard work and they are still doing it today. Yet, while all those girls are caught in the fame/diet cycle, very few will ever admit it in public.

But let's face it, it doesn't take a genius to realise that the only way to be the Perfect Walking Coathanger is by starvation, anorexia or bulimia (and often all three in quick succession). Hey, guess what, fashion world? Older women aren't the only ones with hips, boobs and thighs; young girls have them too!

This is one of those anti-Glama illusions that the Glamazon should never fall for. Those terrible fantasies that can be addictive and a dangerous role model to women of all ages. Ninety-nine per cent of what you see in the fashion magazines is a cleverly manipulated illusion. It's even easier nowadays with computer technology to manipulate the human form into a perfectly toned physique. Not only do most of those cover girls and actresses have fat attacks and bad hair days just like you do, but every one of them has parts of their body that they hate and learn to hide from the world. To add to the illusion, most actresses use body doubles in their films, so the public believes they have a perfect figure. Well they do, but only in monetary form!

When I worked in the modelling game, not one person I worked with (not that I would've taken any notice!) showed any kind of concern to what all this kind of starvation could be doing to my future health. In fact, I was congratulated on my discipline. Luckily for me, I was shocked out of that nonsense at an early age, not through commonsense, but through a combination of vanity and lust (nothing like a dance with a couple of Deadly Sins to bring you back to your senses occasionally!).

I was visiting a very cute guy whom I really fancied. I'd been invited over to his parents' place for a barbecue...well we were only nineteen years old. I thought I looked pretty fabulous stretched out on a sun lounge in my stunning, new bikini—the same one that adorned my wasted frame on that month's cover of Dolly *magazine. I thought I was gorgeous that day, really 'on,' and chatting to everyone and pretending to eat by pushing a few pieces of celery and lettuce around my plate. Suddenly his father, who was big, scary and German, couldn't take it any more. He slapped a massive slab of steak and cream-soaked potatoes under my nose and shouted, 'Eat somesing vill you!! You look ter-ribull!' Pretty mortifying, but he was right.*

Now don't worry, we're not telling you that both of us eat whatever we want and now it's OK to start stuffing your face with foods high in fat and sugar. Balanced, enjoyable eating, combined with regular medium-level exercise is the key. What we're talking about is embracing lots of yummy and naturally healthy foods of all kinds. Throw out all those no-carbs, no-fat and no-dairy diets and all that crap you've been reading in all the magazines and seeing on television talk shows. Glama girls, we know what we're talking about. Read our lips…THEY DON'T WORK! Yes, you will lose weight—temporarily—but you will put it back on again (plus a few kilos more). If anyone knows about stupid crash diets and what it's like to go through years of body angst, it's us. Every woman we know has gone through that. It's a modern phenomenon. And over the years we've both developed our own individual techniques to handle it and to keep a healthy weight range and fitness level.

Look, it's only logical. If you starve your body for more than a week or so, you will drop kilos…well, a lot of fluid, in fact. But if you want to stay slim, stay sane, and stay in the human race (and have some kind of social life), you really need to learn how to eat well, know when your stomach is full, and get some regular exercise. Once you have that breakthrough and learn the keys, it's really not that hard to lose weight and keep a trim shape. A lot of it comes down to attitude and realising that when you learn to listen to your body signals, everything simply falls back into the right body shape and eating pattern. Here are our keys to staying healthy and trim:

- Learn to listen to your body. Your brain, stomach and nervous system is giving you signals all the time so become attuned to them. Look down at your tummy at the dinner table and silently ask: 'Had enough?' Your body is your best friend. It loves you. It is your temple, your golden carriage, and the supercharger that carries you around this incredible planet. Look, listen and learn from it. The 'mind/body' approach recharges and reconnects your body and brain signals and makes listening a cinch.
- Partake in mild exercise, such as stretching or a morning or evening walk. Any form of focused exercise, not just incidental movement like walking over to the fridge or to your car, is vital. It doesn't really matter what kind of exercise you do, just make sure it is something you enjoy and is

at a level where you are more likely to keep it up on a regular basis (at least three to four times a week). Forty minutes to one hour is sufficient to maintain a healthy weight, but even half an hour is one hundred per cent better than no exercise at all. Walk to the beach or your local park, go window shopping, find your local art galleries or visit the curio shops in your neighbourhood, do some pelvic thrusts and butt tucks while watching 'Sex in the City,' or go to an African dance class and get funky and fit in front of that gorgeous instructor.

- Eat three healthy, balanced meals a day.
- Eat smaller portions of high fat and high carbohydrate foods.
- Avoid junk or highly processed food totally. Most foods that can sit on a shelf for months on end contain the kind of chemicals that stuff up your body chemistry.
- Only eat when you are hungry.
- Enjoy the ritual of mealtimes.
- Invest in a personal trainer or see your GP to help you ascertain the right exercises for your level of fitness, age and weight. If you're not into personal trainers or gyms there are lots of reasonably priced DVDs and videos to help you do yoga, pilates or moderate aerobics at home.
- Start your own fitness program by following this simple yet effective body-shaper campaign. Once or twice a week, do a thirty- to forty-minute fast-paced walk either outdoors or on a treadmill followed by a fifteen-minute stretch session. On other days do a thirty-minute session of stretching or yoga plus a thirty-minute fast-paced walk. In summer, you can change the routine to include swimming instead of walking. All this can be done cheaply and on your own or with a Glama pal.
- Finally, accept your body shape—whatever it is. Not every woman is supposed to be as thin as a pin...our hormones simply don't allow it! It's essential to have those womanly curves because they store energy. Did you know that an average woman's body should be twenty-seven per cent fat? So aspire to be toned rather than rake thin.

The Incidental Diva Work-outs

The trick is to do these work-outs at any time of the day whether you're at work or play. Here's how:

- Don't drive to work or to the shops, but if you have to, park your car far enough so you can have a decent walk there and back.
- Whenever you can, choose the stairs instead of the elevator.
- Go out dancing after dinner.
- Go ten-pin bowling—it's retro hip and totally 'now.'
- Try cycling—in stretch capri pants and an Audrey Hepburn headscarf, you'll be stylishly swanning around the city parks in no time.
- Weekend gardening isn't just for grannies anymore. It's now called 'land-scaping' and it's the new craze for getting fresh air and outdoor exercise.
- Do your own DIY home renovations. This 'do it yourself' crafty craze is also great for boosting flexibility and the heart rate.

Glama Calorie Burn-off

Activity	*Calories burned off per hour*
Cha cha or tango lessons	400
Line dancing or hip hop	500
Gardening/landscaping	300–400
Casual window shopping	200 (first day shoe sales—300)
Bowling	220
Boy watching	100
Kissing	135
Sex	200–400 (depending entirely on the pace)

The Lust for Food

Hey, go with it! Did you know that lust is totally lo-cal and a metabolism booster? Of course, it's common knowledge that partaking in various acts of hot sex burns off fat faster than a celebrity Stairmaster (plus a helluva lot more fun), but even spending a lazy hour or two just watching the gorgeous boys (or girls) stroll by and thinking about doing 'it' elevates your heart and metabolic rate. Guess that's why all those sexy Latin lovers manage to stay so slim, even after lazing around coffee bars all day. You can bet that every time those playboys cop an eye-full of a delectable damsel, the lust factor kicks in. The Mediterranean ticker speeds up and straight off the butt goes all that sugar and tiramisu. Well, what better way to stay slim and healthy than to start combining two of the most vital and necessary passions of your life—food and sex. (Coincidently, and quite mystically, both our respective partners are Italians, and both of them are also raffishly slim!)

There is a lot to be said about the Latin culture's age old and fabulously passionate way of approaching both food and love, so why not marry the two passions together? It has worked wonderfully well for most Mediterraneans for thousands of years. It's so obvious and logical, yet somehow, this completely natural approach to the joys of living has become a hidden truth from the rest of the (mainly Western) world—in particular the British, Americans and Australians, where married couples and too many singles are getting fatter, dieting more and shagging less. So viva Italia and *cherche l'amour*!

The Latins follow their nose and listen to their hearts to know what is the best way to eat. It's been scientifically proven that pleasure stimulates the metabolism and helps to maintain overall health and immunity. So listen to your palate and your excess weight will 'miraculously' take care of itself. Go on, be wicked and enjoy every meal and let yourself indulge in what you really love to eat. The Glama secret to a fit and healthy body is to listen to your body signals and not eat unless you are actually hungry.

When you eat, don't just mindlessly wolf down everything on your plate. What a waste of nature's bounty! Enjoy the ritual of mealtimes and the lusty passion of eating tasty food. Even if you're eating alone, set the table, sit down and really savour your food. If you're out to dinner at a restaurant or ordering home-delivered food, look through the menu and select dishes you really feel like. When cooking at home, do the same. Savour the pleasure of waiting to satisfy your desires. When the food is on the table, breathe in the aroma of it—let it stimulate your senses and allow your mouth to water. If you are craving food high in fats, then have it, but in moderation. If you're worried about your weight, just order a smaller portion or take a starter size of your favourite comfort food. You'll be surprised how contented and full you'll feel. This method works because it has the ISF—Incredibly Sinful Factor.

The ISF works because when you eat the opposite of what you really feel like, you won't enjoy it, you won't be satisfied, and your stomach won't turn on its 'I'm full' switch. Your body gets depressed, your metabolism slows down, you still feel hungry and end up bingeing on whatever you have in the fridge. So pay attention to your pleasure zone and eat *what* you like not how *much* you like.

In the world of Glama, miracles can happen. You can still indulge in wicked meals that will add to the passion of feeling full and guilt-free. So tie on that wickedly frilly apron, step into those see-through matching knickers and get baking girl.

But what about the weight conscious Glama girl? The one who enjoys indulgence once in a while but appreciates a well-balanced eating plan. Well, we've picked out some low-fat but completely tasty meals, plus some healthy cooking tips for you.

Healthy Cooking Glamazon Style

Your new diet rule is to embrace the day and enjoy your food. We've picked out the best Glama tips for low-fat cooking and healthier alternatives to all your favourite and sexy Glamazon meals. When cooking Glama style, all you need to do is follow these simple rules to limit your fat intake:

- Bake or grill meat and fish—never fry.
- Select lean cuts of meat when at the butcher.
- Eat milk, yoghurt and cheese for calcium—even the low-fat alternatives still have all the taste.

- Stir-fry vegetables in a little water and salt-reduced soy sauce, so they retain their nutrients and stay crisp.
- Eat lots of fresh fruit and vegetables.
- Use a non-stick frypan.
- Brush the base of your pan with oil, instead of pouring oil into the pan.
- Eat wholemeal bread and cereals instead of fully refined ones.

Hearty Vegetable Soup
Serves four

2 x 400g (13oz) tins crushed tomatoes
2 x 400g (13oz) tins green beans
1 bunch of celery, sliced
2 green capsicums, diced
4 large carrots, sliced
6 small brown onions or a bunch of spring onions, chopped
1 packet of dry soup mix
2 x 400g (13oz) tins low-fat beef or chicken consomme
2 beef or chicken stock cubes
1 tablespoon curry powder
2 cups fresh parsley, chopped
salt and pepper to taste
1 red chilli, chopped (optional)

Place vegetables, soup mix and consomme in a large pot and cover with water. Crumble stock cubes into the soup and stir. Bring soup to the boil, cook for about ten minutes, then reduce to a simmer and continue cooking until the vegetables are tender. This should take about thirty minutes. Make sure you stir the soup occasionally. Add the curry powder and parsley and season with salt and pepper. Allow soup to simmer for a little while longer to allow the flavours to infuse. Add chilli if you like it hot.

Moroccan Lamb Pizza

Serves four

1 tablespoon sunflower oil
1 red (Spanish) onion, finely chopped
1 clove garlic, crushed
225g (7½oz) lean lamb mince
200g (6½oz) tin crushed tomatoes
1 teaspoon ground cumin
1 teaspoon ground coriander
½ teaspoon ground cinnamon
1 tablespoon fresh coriander, chopped
1 tablespoon lemon juice
4 single serves fat-free pizza bases
2 tablespoons pine nuts, toasted
120g (4oz) reduced fat mozzarella, grated
1 cup fresh mint leaves
1 cup fresh flat leaf parsley
cracked black pepper to taste
2 tablespoons mango chutney

Heat the oil in a frypan, add the onion and garlic and cook over a medium heat for one minute. Add the lamb and cook until it is brown, breaking up the meat with a fork. Drain any excess oil from the pan. Add the tomatoes, cumin, ground coriander and cinnamon and cook for five minutes. Stir in the fresh coriander and two teaspoons of lemon juice.

Preheat oven to 200°C (400°F).

Spread the lamb topping over the pizza bases and sprinkle with pine nuts and mozzarella. Bake for ten minutes or until the cheese has melted and the pizzas are heated through.

Toss the mint and parsley leaves in the remaining lemon juice and season with pepper. Serve the pizzas topped with the herb leaves and chutney.

Steamed Snapper with Ginger and Soy

Serves four

1 large snapper, cleaned and scaled
2 tablespoons garlic, crushed
2 tablespoons ginger, crushed
4 tablespoons soy sauce
2 lemons, sliced
freshly ground pepper to taste
2 spring onions, finely chopped on the diagonal

Marinate the snapper with the garlic, ginger and soy sauce for at least two hours in the fridge. Remove snapper from the fridge prior to cooking and place the sliced lemons inside and on top on the fish and season with pepper. To cook the fish, place a round cooling rack in a wok and carefully position the fish on it, or use a fish steamer.

Pour in some boiling water into the base of your steamer or wok, making sure the water doesn't touch the base of the fish. Cover the wok or steamer and steam the fish over a rolling boil for about ten minutes. Test whether the fish is done by flaking a little of the flesh. If it flakes off easily the fish is cooked. Carefully remove the fish from the wok or steamer onto a dish. Sprinkle with spring onions, and garnish with any fresh herb you have handy—dill is the best.

Serve with a healthy green salad.

Shepherd's Pie

Serves four

cooking oil spray
2 brown onions, thinly sliced
1 large carrot, finely chopped
2 celery sticks, finely chopped

500g (1lb) lean chicken mince (if you are vegetarian, opt for lentils)
2 tablespoons plain flour
2 tablespoons tomato paste
2 tablespoons Worcestershire sauce
1 chicken stock cube
500ml (16fl oz) water
1½kg (3lb) potatoes, peeled and cubed
125ml (4fl oz) skim milk
⅓ cup continental parsley, finely chopped
salt and pepper to taste
paprika, for sprinkling

Lightly spray a large non-stick frypan with the cooking oil and heat. Add the onions, carrot and celery and stir until the vegetables start to soften. If they start to stick to the pan add a tablespoon of water. Remove the vegetables from the pan and add the chicken mince. Cook the mince over a high flame until it is well cooked, then add the plain flour and stir for a few minutes. Return the vegetables to the pan and add the tomato paste, Worcestershire sauce, stock cube and water. Bring the mixture to the boil while stirring, then lower the heat and simmer for about twenty minutes. Be sure to stir the meat mixture occasionally to prevent it from sticking.

Meanwhile, prepare the potatoes to make a smooth mash for the pie topping. Place the potatoes in a deep saucepan, cover them with water and boil for twenty minutes or until they are cooked. Strain the water from the pot and mash the potatoes adding a little skim milk until you have the consistency you desire. Set aside.

Return to the mince mixture. Once the mince is cooked, stir the chopped parsley through and season it with salt and pepper. Pour the mixture into a 1½-litre (48fl oz) baking dish and spoon the mashed potato over the top, spreading it evenly with the back of a wet spoon. Roughen up the mash with a fork—this will also give it a bit of crunch.

Sprinkle the topping with paprika and place the dish in the oven or under a grill until the mash turns golden brown and becomes crispy.

Low-fat Fettuccini with Creamy Spinach Sauce

Serves two

500g (1lb) fettuccini
cooking oil spray
2 spring onion stalks, thinly sliced
1 clove garlic, crushed
250g (8oz) fresh baby spinach leaves
375ml (12fl oz) skim milk
2 chicken stock cubes
1 tablespoon cornflour
125ml (4fl oz) water
parmesan cheese, grated to serve

Cook the fettuccini as directed on the pack, while you begin making the sauce.

Spray some oil in a large frypan, add the spring onions and garlic and cook until they are soft and fragrant. Add the spinach leaves and mix well. Add the milk and crumble in the stock. Mix together well. Bring the sauce to the boil, then reduce the heat to a soft simmer. Mix the cornflour with a little water and stir into the sauce.

By this stage the pasta should be cooked. Drain it well and return it to its saucepan. Once the sauce has thickened, add some salt and pepper to taste and mix well.

Place the saucepan containing the pasta over a low heat and pour in the sauce. Add the remaining spring onion and stir through. If the sauce is too dry, add some more skim milk. Serve hot with a sprinkling of parmesan cheese.

Warm Potato and Salmon Salad

Serves four

600g (1lb 3oz) salmon fillet
500g (1lb) new potatoes, halved
cooking oil spray

100g (2½oz) baby corn
100g (2½oz) baby spinach leaves
100g (2½oz) semi-dried tomatoes

Dressing
4 tablespoons reduced fat natural yoghurt
3 tablespoons sweet chilli sauce
2 tablespoons lemon juice

Preheat oven to 200°C (400°F).

Remove the skin from the salmon fillet and then use tweezers to remove any bones. Cut the salmon into large cubes.

Place the potatoes into a large baking dish, lightly spray them with the cooking oil spray and bake for thirty minutes, turning a couple of times during cooking. Add the baby corn to the potatoes and cook for ten minutes or until the potatoes and corn are tender. Turn the oven to low to keep the vegetables warm.

Lightly spray a chargrill with olive oil spray and cook the salmon cubes over a high heat for three to four minutes or until the fish is just tender and golden.

To make the dressing, place the yoghurt, sweet chilli sauce and lemon juice in a small jug and whisk well.

Place the potatoes, corn, spinach and semi-dried tomatoes in a bowl and toss to combine. Arrange the salad on individual plates, top with the hot salmon pieces and drizzle with the dressing to serve.

Cherry Cake
Serves six

cooking oil spray
60g (2oz) self-raising flour
60g (2oz) plain flour
½ teaspoon bicarbonate of soda

1 teaspoon ground cinnamon
1 teaspoon ground nutmeg
125g (4oz) brown sugar, optional
125ml (4fl oz) orange juice
2 egg whites, lightly beaten
250ml (8fl oz) skim milk
410g (13½oz) tin pitted cherries (look for the no added sugar variety)
2 tablespoons icing sugar for dusting, optional

Preheat the oven to 160°C (325°F).

Lightly spray a 23cm (9in) round cake tin with the non-stick cooking spray and line the base with baking paper.

Sift the flours, bicarbonate of soda and spices in a large bowl and add the sugar.

In another bowl, combine the juice, egg whites, milk and cherries. Stir in the flour mixture and mix until thoroughly combined.

Pour the mix into the cake tin and bake for about forty-five minutes. Allow the cake to cool in the tin and then invert it onto a plate and sprinkle with icing sugar.

Guilt-free Chocolate Cake

Serves six

cooking oil spray
185g (6oz) plain flour
60g (2oz) oat flour
220g (7oz) caster sugar
110g (3½oz) unsweetened cocoa powder
2 teaspoons baking soda
375ml (12fl oz) buttermilk
1 egg white
2 teaspoons vanilla essence

Preheat oven to 190°C (375°F). Lightly grease a 23cm (9in) round cake tin with the cooking spray. In a large bowl, combine the plain flour, oat flour, sugar, cocoa powder and baking soda and mix well. In a separate bowl, combine the buttermilk, egg white and vanilla using a whisk. Pour the buttermilk mixture into the flour mixture and combine until smooth. Pour the mix into the cake tin and bake for about thirty minutes or until a knife inserted in the middle of the cake comes out clean. Invert the cake onto a wire rack and allow it to cool.

The Ultimate Diva Temple—the Health Spa

Grab your favourite partner or gal pal and invest some time and money at one of the hundreds of great health and beauty spas around the country.

Whether you book yourself into your local beauty parlour for a couple of hours of pampering, or treat yourself to a day spa or a week at a fabulous health resort, modern day spas are a Glamazon's heavenly haven in so many ways. And many of them are not outrageously expensive, especially considering the long term benefits this kind of investment can bring to your total well-being.

If you're not a health spa convert yet, just give it a go at least once. The next time you have some vacation time coming up, instead of spending a week at the usual kind of hotel resort, book yourself into a different kind of holiday adventure, blissfully devoid of stress, boozy temptations and 'all you can eat' buffets. You won't regret it and you'll be amazed how fantastic you'll look and feel afterwards. A few days at a health retreat is a perfect Glama-girlfriend vacation too. We try to get together regularly for a fun girls-only holiday at one of our favourite Aussie spas—The Golden Door in Queensland. For us, it's become a once a year bonding and beauty ritual. But there are countless other spa retreats around the world that have health and beauty packages, de-tox and naturopathic therapies, glorious deep tissue massages, salty mermaid scrubs and goddess-friendly body treatments of all kinds to re-balance your energies and leave you looking and feeling ten years younger.

'What do I
wear in bed?
Why Chanel No. 5,
of course.'

Marilyn Monroe

Chapter Seven

CLEAVAGE IS A GIRL'S BEST FRIEND

The 'noughties' will be remembered for making the bum crack the new cleavage. While this is definitely a fashion trend, the jury is still out on whether it's actually glamorous. However, cleavage created from pert breasts never goes out of style— it is a magnificent piece of human sculpture that is priceless. When you've got cleavage you've got goddess power and that is the most powerful scent of magic and femininity in the universe. Nothing can top it, so never forget the value of having a good full-bosomed cleavage. So if you're lucky enough to be born with exactly the right boobs to set the world on fire, congratulate yourself. You're already on the way to Glamazon status and best of all, this gift came naturally from Venus, who was obviously smiling on the day you were born.

What you choose to wear to show off your cleavage can also make the difference between being a success or failure in the Glamazon stakes. Wear sexy clothes or accessories that hint boldly or discreetly at sexiness. You don't have to necessarily wear see-through garments or go into sleazeville to make a big impression on the world at large—there's all kinds of ways of hinting at your Glamazon appeal. Donning the kind of dresses, blouses, sweaters and colours (think Kim Novak) that highlight the bosom area, can lay a mental suggestive trail that leads directly to your cleavage. While it isn't necessary to spell it out in neon lights that you've got huge boobs (like Pamela Anderson—although it does seem to have worked for her!), you can definitely, with practise, become a master at using your cleavage power.

But what do you do if you don't have a decent cleavage and you want one? The message here is, if you want to get ahead in life and be a real Glamazon, then you'll need to create one. Fortunately, there are ways to improve your breast power that have transformed many a maiden's dull worldly existence into a full-time heavenly party existence.

Help, My Cleavage is Missing!

The Miracle Bra...it can change your life! This is a piece of architectural gold in terms of under-attire. Known under other names, such as the Push-up Bra or the Wonder Bra, it is certainly not called 'the miracle bra' for nothing! It creates a miracle, indeed, when it uplifts your bosom and projects it outward, like magic. Easy to find, you can venture into any lingerie shop or department store and discover that these bras have the capacity to instantly raise your Glamazon stakes (not to mention your self-confidence) onto a higher level. This investment in your Glama future certainly is a positive step up from being shapeless, saggy or stringy around the bosom area (and much cheaper and easier than a boob job!). While breast implants are costly and a permanent choice for cleavage, this one purchase of a miracle bra (and they come in various lifts, shapes and pertness), can change your life in an instant. To show it off, you may have to make additional purchases too. You may need to buy some fantastic dresses, tops and tight sweaters to display your new assets and you may need to promenade in front of the mirror to check out your new 'cleavage posture.' While having boobs is one thing, knowing how to stand, sit or seductively move, in order to show off your new assets to advantage, is something that takes a little time and energy (but it's well worth the effort!).

Posture

Your mother was right—stand up straight and quit slouching! In order to show off your boobs to full advantage, you need to learn to sit straight. It's a shame that plenty of well-endowed gals sit hunched over, consequently covering up what they should be showing up. Even if they do have the perfect upright and perky boobs of the century, nobody else would ever know it, unless they happen to be laying in bed beside them when they are naked and their pert nipples are gaily pointing up to the ceiling. There are so many gals out there who have an incredible asset in their armory of femininity, but they don't make the most of them. Not only do they hunch over, but they have a tendency to cross their arms when they are sitting down as well. What a mistake! It's like having money in the bank and not investing it. The passage of time combined with inflation will simply waste their wonderful asset away. Tragically, one day Ms Perfect Boobs will wake up and her sex appeal ratio of ten for boobs will have sagged to a five...and she hasn't even been bright enough to cash in on their appeal. So if you've got great boobs, don't be shy—flaunt them! The goddess Venus will reward you if you do. Boobs come under her domain and because she handed them over to you as a gift at your birth, be warned—Venus doesn't like to be scorned. If you don't use them, you'll soon lose them.

Stiletto Power

Have you ever considered why stilettos are so sexy and fabulous? They not only lift you up and give your legs a shapely turn, but they automatically thrust the top half of your body forward. If you want to make the most of your cleavage, then get yourself a serious stiletto collection. Focus on a sexy brand of shoe, such as Manolo Blahniks (he's a master of designing the ultimate sexy shoe), where you can get toe cleavage as well.

What's good for your calves is also good for your cleavage. The stiletto is designed so that it is almost impossible to walk or move without pushing out your cleavage. When you are wearing stilettos, as a side-benefit to your overall look, your bosom just seems to rise and shine. You literally move your body into 'cleavage display' mode and automatically push out your new best assets along with your new stiletto-clad fashion statement.

And So It Is Written: 'Beautiful Cleavage is Not Owned by Girls with Huge Knockers'

Small breasts have always been admired by gentlemen throughout the ages. The 18th century inventors of the champagne glass (which still delicately cups one of the most popular and famous tipplers of glamour) modelled its shape on the young Marie Antoinette's infamous and wickedly teeny bosom. By the 20th century, there still existed connoisseurs of the small but perfectly formed breast—including the owner of Sydney's famous Martin's Bar of the seventies and eighties. The enigmatic Martin, who stood as doorman outside his beloved wine bar every night for twenty years, could remember the first name of everyone who walked through the door of the trendy, avant-garde establishment. His other amazing talent was being able to spot his favourite A-cup bosom from 100 paces away—even those swathed in the most shapeless layers of a goat's wool poncho. The nubile owners of these little wonders would miraculously appear a few nights later, happily employed behind the bar as near topless bar staff—the 'near' being completely see-through gypsy blouses. It could've been seedy, but instead, their nymph-like modesty was protected by great lighting—and who doesn't look stunning behind the pinkish/golden hue of flickering candlelight? The fact is that in the seventies baring your breasts was a political statement, and these brave young divas were looked on as bohemian goddesses. Many of them were university students, poets or budding young artists (excuse the pun).

Small, perky breasts were also a favourite of seventies photographer, David Hamilton, whose misty, soft focus calendar shots of teenage girls were the staple wall decoration of the most fashionable men and women of the time. Today, even amongst the pneumatic Pamela Anderson look-alikes, sexy singer Shakira sings loudly and proudly about her small 'n' humble breasts and both J.Lo's and Kate Hudson's schoolgirl cleavages are shown off beautifully in their silky Versace halter dresses slashed to below the waist—a look only an A- or mini B-cup can stylishly get away with.

And Finally,
Let's Not Forget Nipple Power!

Many Glama gals have sat and pondered the age-old question: should I or shouldn't I put my sexuality out into the marketplace and allow my nipples to perkily push up through my t-shirt or peer through sheer translucent attire? These days, the nipple 'yes or no' question seems to have been replaced with a glimpse of thong underwear instead (we're looking forward to seeing that look bite the dust!), or the terribly hard choice of knowing how much one should expose of various body piercings or tattoos. (Sheesh! The Glama future could look grim if laser removal doesn't get less painful!) Some of the latter kind of fashion choices may be questionable as to whether they're glamorous, but they're all subject to personal taste or youthful folly. However, it is certainly true that some Glama goddesses can look ultra-classy even in outrageous outfits. The gal who knows how to stylishly and sexily package herself can often use 'nipple power' to raise her Glama stakes, attract a guy and beat the opposition.

But remember, before you put on that skin-tight t-shirt without a bra, know that (like apples) there's always going to be nipples and NIPPLES! Every gal has a different size of nipple, breast and body shape. Some bodies work amazingly well with high exposure of certain body parts, while others don't. While delicate A-cup boobs can look bodacious when pushed up against the fabric of t-shirts or transparent blouses, other more pendulous boobs can sometimes resemble cow udders—not that this form of nipple exposure is necessarily bad. There are oodles of horny guys who are big on large boobs. Look at the popularity of *Penthouse* and *Playboy* magazines. If you want to flaunt your big breasts, you'll need to be super-selective about who you go home with, because the 'I love a big-hooter gal' kind of guy can sometimes be sexual trouble. He's looking for a sexual party—not necessarily the gal he wants to take home as his honey. Sex is one thing; relationships are another. If you want him to see you as a Glamazon girlfriend, and not just as a sex object, it may be better to keep your nipples covered up or reserved for show and tell back at his place. But if he's gorgeous and you're looking to party, trust your instincts and do your 'nipple thing' only if it feels right. If you're looking for much more than a sexual fling, it may be wiser to play harder to get.

'Diamonds are forever, but cleavage is a girl's best friend.'

Athena and Deborah

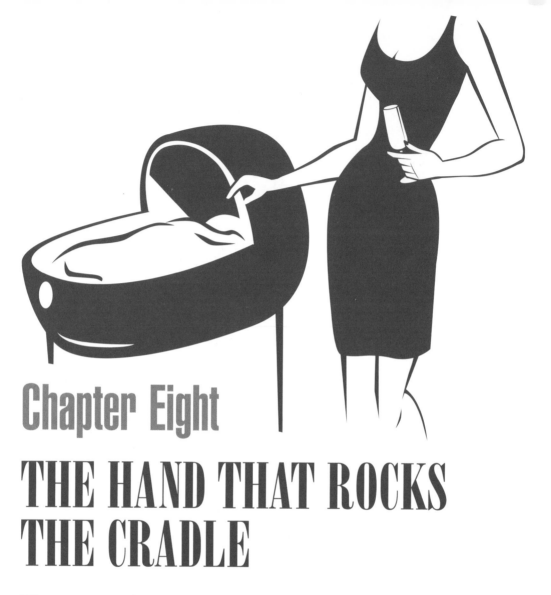

Chapter Eight

THE HAND THAT ROCKS THE CRADLE

When you are a Glamazon (especially if you've landed a fabulous job or the ultimate man to share your Glama universe), you could immediately become the target of other women's envy. Beware of green-eyed monsters, bubble skirts and anti-Glamazons! Envy and dislike may be openly displayed or come at you on psychic or hidden levels, like shadows in the night.

Just about every woman on the planet has experienced female jealousy in one way or another. They've either been the target of it or shelled it out themselves. This view might not be 'politically correct'—it may even get up a few noses to say it—but the truth of the matter is that the more successful your life becomes, the more likely there'll be some other gal out there smouldering with the desire to smother you in your sleep. In fact, the more Glama-fied your life becomes, the stronger her urge will be to sneak into your boudoir de Glama and drown you in your bubble bath. Don't be too shocked. It's a fact of life, and when you think about it, who can truly blame them? After all, anyone who lacks any kind of fulfilment in their life, will never forgive you for having a full-on Glamazon existence. Sure, us modern girls have it all going on. We're loving, nurturing mothers of the Earth and loyal sisters of support, but our equally powerful inner 'dark goddess' seems to have been completely overlooked lately and misread for centuries.

It's perfectly normal that all women have their own ferocious lioness within. It's that fiercely competitive nature (that's either glossed over or totally ignored by most writings on modern sociology and human behaviour), which lurks within all women to protect us, that gives us the tenacity to not only outsmart and out-run men, but also the biological drive to compete with other women. There's nothing wrong with recognising that side of being a woman. In fact, it's vital that you learn to understand it. It's just that when you top up that kind of perfectly natural instinct with a big dose of Glama envy, then you've got a volatile mix that you must always be ready for and aware of.

Now here's the tough part of the equation. Those closest to you can often secretly envy you the most. It's another one of those rules of the Glama universe that some of the most treacherous and traitorous acts can be wreaked upon you by not only your nearest and dearest friends, but—wait for it—even some of your own relatives. Think of Cinderella and her ugly step-sisters—there's more to that fable than just a fairytale—it is an insight into the eternal nature of competitive female behaviour. It will be a rare jewel of a woman who can be your true friend. If you are fortunate enough to find her, she's likely to be another fully-fledged Glamazon who has no need to be envious of you at all (cos she's too busy getting on with her own life to worry about yours!). The level playing field sisters are the only kind of gal pals that you really need in your 'A-team'—and your inner circle. That special group of understanding friends who help you through the tough times, share your joys and triumphs, and keep any of your wine-induced confessions and dastardly mistakes locked up forever in the secret vault of friendship. Sure those type of friends are out there, but you have to learn to recognise which ones are the flowers in your garden and which ones are the noxious weeds. A true Glamazon friend delights in supporting you and seeing you grow from strength to strength, while a green-eyed monster gal will not. It can be lonely being a Glamazon, but keep your wits about you and you'll eventually find pals who truly delight in your success without hating you for it as well.

Competition among men is applauded by society, while in women it's been ignored like a shameful secret. But it's there, and it's been simmering for eons. You've just got to learn to deal with it.

What's Fair in Love and War

When you allow certain kinds of people, either male or female, too much power in your life (or listen to their advice) they'll subliminally or knowingly undermine your prospects. Give them an inch and they will affect your progress in all kinds of ways. They can't help themselves! For some of them it's their job...their total agenda in befriending you! For example, take those catty scheming gal pals or bitchy hairdressers who convince you to try the latest hairstyle that doesn't suit you, or encourage you to cut off your long luxurious sexy locks. Or the so-called gal pal who keeps cancelling your work-out classes together and instead has you sitting around her depressing flat for hours on end commiserating over her latest disastrous relationship while she feeds you tubs of ice-cream and peanut butter sandwiches. (She'll feel so much better when you break out in pimples and stack on a few kilos!)

You'll soon discover that certain kinds of men and women will do their best to sabotage you, with the loser males doing their best to downgrade your confidence, run off with your savings or screw your best friend. While the anti-Glamazons are busily trying to sabotage your self-esteem, sex appeal or marriage. You need to keep your eyes wide open to avoid being ambushed. Most anti-Glamazons, though, are easy to spot and can usually be avoided. These are the girls who will get you into trouble as quickly as they can, given half a chance. So be warned in advance, and be ready to recognise them. Beware of those who:

- Think it is attractive to smell 'au naturelle' and don't wear deodorant.
- Think underarm hair is even more attractive than leg hair.
- Think wearing make-up is stupid, sinful, dirty, cheap and nasty.
- Always look as though they've just dragged themselves out of an unmade bed.
- Figure it is easier and speedier to get themselves a guy by falling pregnant, and end up making a career out of having several children to several fathers.
- Blame their ongoing bad fortune on everyone else but themselves.
- Carry a huge chip on their shoulder.

With these gals, whatever you do, don't make the fatal mistake of feeling sorry for them. In their own sick way, they are experts at manipulation and all kinds of guilt trips and emotional blackmail, and often make their way through life by being specialists at loading others up with passive–aggressive mind games. When, and if, you do spot one trying to manoeuvre her way into your life and business, your best advice is to start rapidly moving in the opposite direction. Now while these first anti-Glamazon gals are easy to spot, they aren't the only gals you need to watch out for. There's a whole other breed of Glama-envious chicks out there who are cleverly disguised and much tougher to pick. These are the gals who may look like Glamazons themselves, but are actually imitations of the real thing. Of all the gals you need to watch out for, it is these phoney Glamazons that can cause you the most grief and trouble. They're usually those girls who start off incredibly sweet and flattering towards you and are always asking to borrow your clothes or use your make-up. Then one day they spookily turn up to a social event in your exact same outfit and hairstyle—in every detail. They become obsessive with following your every look and move. They push that old cliché 'imitation is the sincerest form of flattery' to the extreme, so that even your lover starts to mistake her for you. (Starting to get the picture?) We've met a few of these little gems ourselves in our travels, and believe us, these are the lethally dangerous compe-titors you will face because you don't realise what they're up to until they have caused you extreme angst. If you want to know what these gals are capable of, go and rent the old classic flick with Bette Davis called *All About Eve*, or watch the absolute extreme of cases in the more recent movie *Single White Female*. The sooner you realise that you need to be your own best friend and adviser, the better. Trust yourself first, then work on building your own strong Glama-team of genuine pals.

Wonder Weddings

Go girl! You've landed your perfect man and now you're planning the wedding of the century. For this—one of the most important days of your life—every Glama girl should ensure she chooses the perfect time and day of the week. Although there are many factors to consider for the big day, such as work commitments, the perfect season for fine weather, availability of your bridesmaids and overseas guests, and, of course, whether your favourite church and reception centre is free, does the day you marry influence your marriage future? Does it help to bring about a successful wedding or even add to the essence of the pairing and marriage? Why be just one of the weekend crowd when you can marry on any day of the week? Glamazons should know how to think outside the giftbox.

Once you've cosmically connected with the perfect wedding planner and you've started choosing from all the different new and old wedding traditions, how about considering some other age-old traditions, such as ensuring you're aligning yourself with the most magical and fortuitous days in your Glama calendar? One of the best ways of doing this is to choose the luckiest times of the week that will be an exact fit for both your personality and relationship needs. Well, you've come this far on the Glamazon trail, so why not use every-thing at your disposal to help make sure that yours is one of the most beautiful, fabulous and glamorous weddings ever.

Every day of the week has its own unique energy field. Each has its own planetary vibration that puts a kind of cosmic canopy over the marriage, which exerts a continuing influence for the years ahead. First, think about your expectations for the marriage. Consider all the greatest hopes you have for your relationship and lifelong partnership. Write down a few points in a notebook and read through them a few times. Then, take a look through the following list to find your perfect Glama day for a long and happy marriage.

Monday: A Soul Marriage

Is the ultimate soul connection, emotional sensitivity and understanding the most important factor in your partnership? If so, then Monday would be your perfect wedding day. Monday is ruled by the Moon—Moonday—and is symbolically represented by a bear.

Monday weddings are always fun, as well as intensely deep and introspective. Monday weddings might have an appearance of being high-spirited, but you can bet the partners are walking on an emotional tightrope beneath their controlled exterior.

Throughout the course of their married life, the partners of a Monday wedding will experience phases in their relationship like the waxing and waning of the Moon itself. At times they will be inseparable, or they will take turns to sulk and perhaps need some time out from each other for rest and reflection.

The Moon is the ruler of changes; it also pulls the emotional tides. This indicates a Monday marriage will fluctuate, sometimes drastically. Outsiders looking on would be confused by the extremes of tenderness and love operating alongside such moodiness. Sensitivity is very important in this relationship, with the slightest criticism being taken seriously and cutting to the quick. But there is a special quality about a Monday wedding if the partners can overcome the emotional sensitivity. With awareness there is a great depth of soul love behind this marriage. The Moon can link two people together on this level. If they open up to each other fully and are very honest, this can give them the ability to tune into each other's moods and feelings. It will be easy for these partners to become jealous and possessive of each other, so care needs to be taken not to become co-dependent.

As the Moon rules children, family and home affairs, these will be the focus of attention for those married on a Monday. Children born of this marriage will be more psychic and emotional in outlook than usual. Residing close to the sea's energy field would prove very therapeutic for both parents and children. It is also likely that a mother or mother-in-law will make an impact upon this marriage, as she also comes under the rulership of the Moon.

A Monday marriage lays a great foundation for a romantic and emotional life-time together. With the Moon being a reflecting planet, this symbolises that the partners of this marriage will eventually receive back the same energy they put out. The two partners will reflect each other in many ways and may even begin to 'look alike' over the period they spend together. If they can rise above pettiness, jealousy and possessiveness, these Moon-influenced partners have a wonderful opportunity to create a close soul contact, which will be more connected than most marriages around.

Tuesday: A Challenging Marriage

Do you bore easily and are both looking for an exciting and challenging life and marriage? Then Tuesday is your day for wedding plans. Tuesday is ruled by the planet Mars, and is symbolically represented by the arrowhead.

Marrying on this day is highly suited to the couple who love to live an exciting life together and enjoy sharing and taking on challenges. For the day itself, with Mars ruling your wedding day, this is going to be an action-packed, dramatic, exciting union, but it is wise to expect a few bumps and bruises along the way. There will be nothing dull, boring or routine about this marriage. Astrologically, Mars means energy—energy of a volatile, explosive kind. Where relationships are concerned, Mars will charge them up. This means there will be plenty of energy, passion and interaction between you and your partner. But Mars has powerful energy, so watch out for explosive outbursts and try to avoid aggression and aiming to always be the winner in an argument.

Mars also rules impulsive behaviour, so it may be that this wedding is likely to have something 'rushed' and spontaneous about it. It will be a high energy occasion.

Through the lifetime of the marriage, 'drama' will be its keyword. If you want a tranquil existence, choose another day of the week to marry! If you like excitement marry on this day, but have lots of outside activities so you can let off steam outside of the union. Sport and career are likely to play a big role in this marriage. Sex and any sort of physical pastime will be a big part of the energy exchange between you (sex and sport are ruled by Mars too). Sex in this marriage can become the perfect stress release between both partners.

Children born from this marriage are likely to be strong-willed and assertive and even a bit rebellious. Their fast past could make them great at all kinds of sports, and it is not unlikely that they will come home with bumps and scratches and even a broken limb from a touch football or rowdy play session occasionally.

As Mars rules the masculine side of the individual, ego and strength of will plays a big role in this relationship. So it would be wise to sort out who is in charge of which areas of the partnership and agree to take turns at being 'the one on top.' There will be healthy competition between both partners if they are involved in business together. But even if problems arise, one partner needs to play the role of arbitrator and talk things through. Power struggles can easily erupt if one attempts to organise the other's affairs, so ensure an understanding is reached early in the marriage. Upheaval could erupt over trivia because spirits are high here, but compassion and compromise will soothe any storms away. But consider all the great sex that follows any silly flare up!

A marriage that takes place on a Tuesday is designed for the ambitious, high energy couple who thrive on drama. If your ideal marriage is one based on tranquillity, it is wise to marry on another day. Yet for those who love a challenge and to learn something new every day, Tuesday weddings should be your Glama choice.

Wednesday: An Active Marriage

Are you and your partner the eternal 'Peter Pans'—never really wanting to shed the magic of your childhood? If so, then a Wednesday wedding will help keep the youth and spontaneity alive in your marriage. Wednesday is ruled by the planet Mercury and is symbolically represented by the triskele—a figure consisting of three legs emanating from a common centre.

A Wednesday marriage will have all the ingredients needed to keep the partners 'young at heart.' There will always be excitement in the air, but it is most important that the couple be able to express their thoughts and feelings very easily with each other. With the planet Mercury ruling Wednesday, a marriage commenced on this day will be certain to develop into a fast-moving, mentally stimulating relationship. Mercury rules the mind and the speed of thought, so this marriage is destined not to stand still. Both partners should be a good match mentally, otherwise one will be left behind by the other, who will want to grow and go through all sorts of adventures to learn new things.

Anything operating under Mercury's domain cannot accept the restriction of routine. Consequently, a Wednesday marriage will need to undergo constant changes to remain fulfilling. It is necessary that both partners be prepared to seek out whatever is new and stimulating to them and incorporate it within the structure of the marriage. One of the highlights of this marriage will be the capacity of both partners to explore anything and everything together with a shared delight and curiosity. Consequently these marriage partners will always remain children at heart.

There will always be humour in this union and the partners will have a great sense of fun. A busy social life should be part and parcel of their lives, with much contact with brothers, sisters and other immediate family members. It is likely that a great deal of travelling will take place, although this may be over short distances (particularly interstate) on a frequent basis.

Both partners will desire constant involvement in interests outside of the marriage to provide an input into the life they share together at home. It would be unhealthy for this couple to watch too much television because this will eat up their creative energy, which would be wonderful to expand upon together. Communication is vital, so it is likely that this couple both spend a lot of time on the phone either talking to each other, or others. Their home will be filled with gizmos and gadgets and they will be up to date with the latest electronic goods or computer features. Interests that occupy the mind, such as chess, card games, backgammon and other competitive 'mind games' are likely to be pastimes.

Children born of this marriage will sometimes have delicate features and love to read and be around nature. But even if they are oversensitive and rather shy, the

Mercury-influenced children will grow stronger as they develop. They will have great minds, be quick learners and anxious participants in every family discussion.

Partners of a Wednesday marriage can tend to be mental butterflies, sometimes looking for stimulus from the most unexpected quarters. Career is important, as it provides a happier and healthier frame of mind once it is fulfilling, and the marriage benefits from both partners working. Wednesday marriages assure that there will never be a dull moment.

Thursday: An Indulgent and Rich Marriage

Perhaps financial security and a rich, prosperous life is your key to a happy partnership. If so, then Thursday may supply your pot of gold. Thursday is ruled by the planet Jupiter, and is symbolically represented by the symbol of a hammer or a flyfot cross (a cross with each tine bent at ninety degrees in a counter-clockwise direction).

With the benevolent Jupiter ruling Thursday, this is quite a 'lucky day' for marriages. Good fortune smiles on Thursday (maybe that's got something to do with it often being payday!) Abundance, good times and all of life's pleasures should be the rewards of those who marry on this day. However, like all abundance and plenty, sometimes too much of a good thing can become quite boring and gets taken for granted. Unfortunately that sometimes happens to the marriages made on this day—they become stagnant and boring, but only because of lack of input from the marriage partners who simply stop making any attempt to keep things exciting. They tend to 'become lazy' at loving and everything else happening in the marriage.

Jupiter provides protection for good health too, and as this planet also rules the sign of Sagittarius, it provides a sense of vision to the marriage, making opportunities for the future. Both partners in this marriage will develop a keen feeling for 'speculation.' They will also become more confident because of their marriage and may be taken on adventurous pastimes together.

Money can be overspent quite easily with a Thursday marriage. Financial dealings need careful supervision. Jupiter can encourage overindulgence and it is possible to not only overspend, but to over-drink and eat as well. 'Optimism' is their keyword but they can carry this to an extreme, for example, going on an expensive holiday at a time when they need to conserve funds.

This couple must beware of developing an attitude within the marriage of 'me' first and 'you' second. Sometimes sharing is a difficult thing to do when your interests begin and end with your own desires and needs. That's one thing Jupiter will teach the couple who become entrapped in such selfish desire—abundance and options can disappear overnight and it is important to balance the marriage emotionally and make sure they spread their good fortune around!

Children born of this marriage will be appealing and easy to spoil, although when young, they may be a tad lazy regarding their school studies. When they grow older their range of interests will expand and they will often turn around and become involved in all kinds of activities or sport.

A marriage commenced on a Thursday is destined to be a happy one, although should personality differences arise, it is good to make sure that neither partner avoids confrontation to the point where they'd rather just keep problems to themselves. A fighting spirit is often not very strongly developed in a Thursday marriage, so it's wise to also balance any problems with maturity so you avoid the 'it hasn't worked, just let's call it a day' attitude. But if you put a little effort into a Thursday marriage you usually end up very happy, healthy and content!

Friday: A Love Marriage

Since you were a little girl you've been dreaming of your Prince Charming—your true love. If you're both true romantics and love doves, then Friday's goddess of Venus will shine her passion on your union. Friday is ruled by the planet Venus and is symbolically represented by the Cross Pattee-Nowy (a cross with four equal arms that expand in width outwards).

Love is a knee-trembling, heart-thumping affair whenever Venus and her lovechild Cupid are involved. Weddings performed on a Friday come under the domain of Venus, so if the stars are likely to shine in the eyes of a loving couple, you'd expect this from a Friday marriage. Romance and all its trappings are the very spices that Venus uses to flavour her love spells.

There is a star-struck youthful quality to Venus' influence over lovers. Venus represents an intensely female energy force—she influences the female side of the psyche...the deep mystery of womanhood, which is also a very difficult, mysterious depth to fathom. Her female traits are incredible strength, but also intense vulnerability and all these qualities are brought into a Friday marriage. Venus also delights in bringing into a marriage the worst of all the female foibles—bitchiness towards her partner. This is the type of union that is boiling when it's hot, but when it is cold, it is icy cold. The cycles of infatuation and resentment can run rampant because of the romantic illusions that often go hand-in-hand with this relationship structure.

For those couples who aren't smitten by Venus' overwhelming promises of a 'happy ever after' fantasy, a Friday wedding is guaranteed to be a love affair to remember. Provided the newlyweds keep a level head when changing their fantasies into future plans, everything should continue to bring even more love into their lives.

When Venus is involved in a relationship, she demands plenty of attention and will go to any length to keep that attention coming her way—even if it involves the partners creating dramas, or behaving outrageously just to stir up jealousy or receive more attention from their partner.

Children born of this union will have a special type of beauty—a magical form of charisma. They are also likely to be talented. Music and creativity will be their special gifts and, if encouraged, they could end up making a livelihood from the arts. At an early age they will be extremely fashion conscious, knowing exactly what they want to wear (sounds like the perfect mini-Glamazon!). They will also have a loving nature and will stand out in the crowd, as if they have a shining light surrounding them.

Where marriage is concerned, Friday has definite advantages and disadvantages. Venus' influence can alter like the flip of a coin, so like the little girl who had the little curl...when the marriage is good it will be very good, but try not to be too horrid! Venus rules affection, beauty, friendship, pleasure, sensuality, good living, eroticism, magnetic attraction, peace, sympathy and perception...which undoubtedly are all wonderful ingredients to create a loving marriage. Where both partners can rise above selfishness of the narcissistic kind, they will adore each other like sweethearts of adolescent days.

Saturday: A Testing but Rewarding Marriage

If your road to marriage has been a long struggle to find the perfect match, then you will both appreciate the deep meanings of destiny and the eternal commitment that Saturday can bring to a strong, rewarding relationship. Saturday is ruled by the planet Saturn—Saturnday. The day is symbolised by the sickle.

Astrologically, Saturn is the Grim Reaper, the Old Man of Time. He teaches patience, perseverance and the meaning of perfecting character through trial and error. If this sounds heavy going, it is—especially when you decide to marry on the very day where his influence prevails.

Marrying on a Saturday symbolically places a couple at the foot of a climb up the highest mountain. 'Happiness' awaits at its peak, beckoning temptingly, but a lot of effort, energy and dedication is needed to reach this goal. The 'happiness' to be found at the top of Saturn's mountain is far greater than that offered by the other planets, and to reach it requires total commitment. Any pitfalls and crossroads that lead to this 'fulfilment' can build true bonds between partners. For those married on a Saturday, the strong and steadfast couple will find the pot of gold that awaits them.

Children born of a Saturday marriage are children of destiny. They reflect the karma of the partner's previous lives and often are similar to their grandparents or some other family member of the past. Their addition to the family circle either creates a closer bond between the partners, or a rift. The children themselves seem older and wiser than their years and have the ability to absorb the feelings of others around them. They have an inherent ability to understand other people's problems and are often referred to as 'having old heads on young shoulders.' They are frequently very visionary.

To marry on a Saturday requires real commitment, will and discipline. It demands that each partner knows that besides love, it takes work and focus to create a successful marriage. They should give each other compassion and understanding without hesitation and always assume the role of helper and supporter. Saturday marriages require unconditional love and surrender. The protective energy field that will propel a Saturday marriage to great success and longevity is unconditional love. In this day and age, where life flows merrily along in most quarters, not too many people are prepared to put themselves out unconditionally. Consequently, if you are prepared to give your 'all' to the marriage, then get married on a Saturday.

Sunday: A Powerful Marriage

If you wish to keep a spark of your independent nature but still be worshipped like the Sun Goddess, then Sunday is the most illustrious day for you both to shine on into luminous matrimony. Sunday is the day of the Sun and is symbolised by the solar rays from the head of the Sun God.

Astrologically, Sunday is a very good day for marriage, because it is ruled by the Sun and the Sun itself knows no limitation—it promotes growth, activity, energy, passion, ego, freewill and accomplishment. Sunday became known as Gods Day because its special energy made it so attractive that the Gods chose this day to claim it for themselves. Whenever the Sun's cosmic energies surround or influence a wedding, it sends out a special blessing. Therefore marrying on a Sunday provides a celestial spark, pushing the partners forward, encouraging them to do a lot of things they would probably never think about doing if they weren't together. The Sun energises and enthuses the marriage, but what the partners do with this energy is also up to them. They can make more or less of it.

The very essence of the sun is 'life' and consequently whatever crises a marriage celebrated on a Sunday should face will eventually lead to a new life or growth of some kind. There will be a special bond between the people who marry on a Sunday. A Sunday marriage could easily turn into a spiritual union, for what happens when people marry on a Sunday is their spirits get merged together by the influence of the Sun—it melts them into oneness.

Naturally there will be some disillusioned marriages forged on a Sunday because the Sun also rules Ego, so the personality clashes and desire factor will be strong in this union. Ego often makes people behave badly to one another and competition of some kind could erupt. It is difficult for people who are fixed in their ways to alter under the sun's influence—they want things done 'their way.' If such a situation arises, conflicts could manifest where both parties have strong leadership qualities and neither one wants to be the follower. A Sunday marriage usually unites two very independent people and the proper application for this situation is not for them to keep assuming their individual leadership in the marriage, but to carefully delegate which areas they are both in control of and to respect this.

Children born from a Sunday marriage are independent and self-assertive from an early age. They seem quite capable of looking after themselves. They have great respect and love for their parents (particularly the father). They are unafraid and brave, but can also be quite cheeky and rebellious at school if they are not taught to respect other people and authority figures.

A Sunday wedding provides the marriage partners with an open book to write their own joint marriage story. All the ingredients are given to them to play with by the patron of their marriage day, the Sun. However the success of the marriage will depend on each partner's actions and openness to change and growth (similar to the world's seasons) throughout the years of the union. When you marry on a Sunday you are given the role of self-creator. This is not only one of the biggest responsibilities, but also one of the greatest gifts of all. It depends totally on your attitude and inner strengths and weaknesses.

House Rules

So here you are—congratulations! By your own dedication, focus and psychic energies you've succeeded where other women have failed. You're a Glamamama. Not only have you established your wonderland but, at long last, you're sharing your fabulous life with a handsome husband/partner. You entertain and enjoy living in your great home. Your children are gorgeous and healthy and all seems well with your world...so what can still go wrong? Plenty! Now that you've achieved success, watch out for anyone who sets their sights on what you have and who will go to any underhanded means to get it. Naturally you can't fend off all the girls who will want what you have (because that is just about everybody of the fairer sex in the world!), and because your husband/partner has to venture forth into the wide world on his own at times, un-chaperoned by you (unfortunately), you can't always keep other women's hands off him. But one thing you can do is control who comes and goes into your home.

The biggest threat to any Glamazon homemaker may very well be the staff she has working for her at her Casa de Glama. Too quickly those seemingly helpful employees can become too intimate with not only you and your children but, horror of all horrors, your husband as well. Before you know it, that nubile nanny of yours has moved the eager friendliness onto a whole new level, where it becomes sexual intimacy with your husband/partner. And you think we're exaggerating just a tad? Well, what does your babysitter get up to when you're not around? Picture it. You're stuck back at the office one night in a long drawn-out meeting, while that sixteen-year-old next door neighbour has just plonked her luscious butt onto your brand new Versace sofa in her micro-mini, crossing and uncrossing her legs. Your two-year-old innocently plays like a puppy at her feet and your husband sits nearby, relaxing after a hard day at work, martini in hand, panting like a dog. You think this is a rare situation? Hello? What are you thinking, girl! Don't kid yourself. This very scenario has been a major disaster for many a blissful household. You cannot underestimate the power or danger (even life-threatening) of some wannabe Glama working right in the centre of your hearth and home. Consider as an example the movie *The Hand that Rocks the Cradle*, and those of you who haven't seen it, go and get it on video. Rebecca De Mornay plays a revengeful role and ends up almost killing the heroine who allows her into her home to play nanny. Even if you haven't seen the movie, you don't want to let any Rebecca De Mornays into your palace. Any switched-on woman who reads the newspapers, watches the television or regularly chats to other smart Glamazons knows that it is the babysitter, the au pair, the nanny, the personal assistant, the housekeeper, the secretary, the female fitness instructor, or even the wedding planner, who often ends up having hanky-panky with the man of the house. She replaces the mistress of the house (you!) and plays the role of the princess herself, which naturally was her plan right from the beginning!

On the other side of the gold coin, this insightful info can be used to great advantage for the Glama babe-in-the-making. The role of nanny, au pair, secretary and personal assistant are often fabulous for any Glamazon-in-training to assume—especially a Glamazon who still hasn't found her romantic, financial or security niche, and wants one or all of them. However, for the Glamazon who has found it all and is with her ideal man, has children, is currently languishing in her Casa de Fabulous and enjoying her hard earned trappings—without any exceptions whatsoever (even if the most appealing case appears who totally fits the agenda for the job on offer), it is wise for her to always consider the other woman playing key roles in the family's existence.

Certainly no other female figure or 'free spirit' with even a whiff of sexuality, a dash of cute friendliness, any kind of girl-next-door appeal, or a delightful 'sense of humour' should be allowed to play any role in the running, maintenance or upkeep of the Glamazon's family or work areas. Even if this person is doing the most simple tasks, like polishing your silver, be assured that if your husband's a keeper, give her a chance and she'll be polishing off more than your antique spoons.

Just look around and see how some deranged women actually invite and allow some little conniving nymphet cunningly disguised as a nanny or an au pair into their home. You immediately know that foolish woman is flirting with potential disaster and you can bet she'll pay a high price for it. One of the gals who is most successful in winning the Mercedes sports car, the several holiday homes around the world, the luxury yacht, and the husband away from the Glamazon (as well as the children), is the conniving nanny. Of all the enemies you can invite into your home, it is the nanny who seems to be able to manipulate situations to her advantage the most successfully. Somehow this gal seems to have an innate knack of getting everything you've got and leaving you screwed, big time.

So if you must have an au pair or housekeeper, employ an old and ugly one. Never underestimate the power a young nanny will yield in your home. What you think is not presentable, others may find most attractive, so make sure she's a little bit cranky to boot so nobody really likes her that much. Think Hunchback of Notre Dame; think Nurse Ratched. Search the planet for Mrs Doubtfire. Yes, she'll do a very good, efficient job, but she could never be indispensable (that's your job after all), and your husband/partner would barf up his lunch if she ever made a pass at him. You must never ever employ anyone who is in any way passible as a lover and girlfriend. Often, just being in a position to wield some power over the people around them is all some women need to get what they want. Remember, you want them to housekeep, not keep the house!

If you must have staff, try to make them men. If they can't be men, then choose much older women with plenty of teenage or grown-up kids themselves. That way, she'll be too exhausted and 'over it' to want yours. Be selective and smart. Yes, it may sound paranoid, but that's how you'll remain queen of the realm. Give an inch and you could lose the lot.

POSITION VACANT

Totally unattractive elderly nanny required to supervise two absolutely purr-fect children. Nymphets need not apply.

The Queen of the Castle
(who intends to stay that way)

Chapter Nine

VIVA COSMETICA

We once saw this headline on the cover of a magazine—'Always be yourself.' Well, yeah, what else can you be? Even when you're 'faking' it, it still must be your own unique version of faking! Besides, just how many different 'you's' do you have? Think about it. As you mature from a young girl into a grown woman, it becomes almost mind-boggling how many sides of your personality you discover. Perhaps the headline should've read—'Be all that's you.' All two hundred and seventy-seven sides (so far) or whatever number comes close. Women are like brave explorers, trekking around the world of our true natures, discovering new territories, claiming unknown characters, and crossing over mountain ranges of unforeseen reactions.

Celebrities too have scores of personalities, only theirs have the perfect shoes and bag to match! Just about all of the most famous chicks around know about the changing and mutably magnetic icons of eternal female power. The cleverest celebrities also have teams of the most talented hair stylists and cosmetic artists on the planet to help make-up every one of those personalities into spellbinding perfection. Think of the numero uno celebrities who have cottoned on to all the archetypes of beauty and glamour to keep their careers alive. Madonna has managed to go from bullet bras to Buckingham Palace, with a different iconic face and hair colour to go with every sensational occasion. She has modelled her persona on the allure of many past Glamazons and Glama styles—Marilyn Monroe, Eva Péron, 1930s Hollywood glamour à la Jean Harlow, Japanese geishas and every look from a virgin to a vamp—all through the magic of make-up. Then there's Kylie with her girl next-door curls and lip gloss, who set her career in locomotion as everything from a pale rock goddess to a shimmery gold disco babe. J.Lo— Jenny from the block—was born with a high fashion upper torso and a porn star ass. Does she get confused when dressing up her two opposite sides? And how many of her lucky boyfriends gets to experience both her Glama divas on the same night? The list goes on and on.

A Glamazon from the past, Grace Kelly, was the divine Princess of Ice who wore white gloves along with the most stylish and coolly blonde bob. But it's also a well-documented fact that behind closed doors, her men were shown a hot-blooded temptress. We can assure you that Ms Kelly was not only dressed accordingly, but she also used the ancient art of cosmetics to reveal the sweet virgin or the sexy tart. Well why not? All Glamazons, past and present, know that in this great theatre of life, you need the best make-up and lighting you can find. Of course, for a decent level of happiness and contentment in life, it's essential to be true to the inner you (once you find out what the core of that is!), but the rest of it can be completely Made-Up in this highly visible world of Glama. And you can do all of that without having to employ a full-time entourage. Choose an attitude or take out one of your personalities for dressing up. Choose your favourite clothes and cosmetic colours, and parlay it all into a fabulous and flawless look that's iconic, magical and all your own.

Slather it, slosh it, or slap it on with a trowel; use as much make-up as it takes, just as long as it looks completely natural and spontaneous. Do you wanna stay young forever? Simple. What colour was your hair as a child? Dye it to kingdom come until it matches your hair as a toddler and then you can honestly say, 'This is the colour I was born with.' Yes, your girlish glow may have gone a-wandering for a few years, but now it's miraculously back on track. And you can do all of it without having to employ a celebrity swat team or a full-time entourage. Start by following this easy guide to canny cosmetics.

First the Basics

The secret to fabulous skin is to first pick the right parents...and then do the best with what you've got! Well, actually, the real secret to maintaining healthy skin throughout the years is the Magic Three Technique—cleanse, moisturise and mask. It is essential for every Glamazon to cleanse and moisturise every day with products that suit her skin type. This is the only way she will keep her appearance in top condition. Purchase one mask or peel for deep cleansing and another for deep moisturising and a day moisturising cream or lotion that helps to plump up the skin. (We don't believe in alcohol-filled toners except if you've got really oily skin, but even oily skin can do with a light water-based moisturiser.) There are so many excellent products available—so many, that the subject of skincare could cover another Glama book in itself (stay tuned for *Glamazon Two: Skin-sational!*).

The key is to do your own research in the skin care stakes. One of the best ways is to book an appointment with a reputable beauty salon and get a facial. The beauty technician will be able to analyse your skin type and recommend which products are suited to it. Of course, you don't have to buy everything she says. Instead, incorporate your own preferences and go out and get some free advice from cosmetic counter consultants in your favourite department store. It's up to you to discover what products work for your skin. Many cosmetic companies offer complimentary facials and often have top-level make-up artists and skin care professionals travelling from state to state advising on the skincare and cosmetics in their range and offering priceless tips.

In a nutshell, to keep a clean Glama face is really quite simple—you just have to be disciplined! You need to adopt a daily routine of skin care to help your skin look its best. Use a water-soluble cleanser, so you can wash it off with tepid water, and moisturise with a light cream or lotion. You need to do this twice a day, morning and night. A night cream can be used before going to bed, and an intensive eye cream (not too heavy or your eyes will swell) can be beneficial too. Just apply the cream under your eyes, never on the eyelid. You also need to give your skin a special treatment at least once a week. This means either exfoliating, steaming your face, or using a purifying mask to deep clean your pores. Finally, stick to fragrance- and alcohol-free products—there are many available in all price ranges—and add various age-defying boosters for the neck and eyes once you feel they are required.

Secrets to Younger-looking Skin

Every Glama gal should pull the stops out to maintain a youthful complexion, and this can take a bit of work! But we have some foolproof tips that will guarantee your skin stays soft and wrinkle-free for many years to come:

- Always, always, always use sunscreen to prevent the skin ageing. The sun is largely responsible for wrinkling, liver spots, the thinning of the skin, broken blood vessels, dryness, changes in texture, uneven colour and skin diseases such as melanoma. Use a sunscreen daily (at least SPF15[+]), along with protective clothing such as hats when you go out into the sun. Sunglasses will also protect the eyelids from ageing by helping to reduce the crows feet produced by squinting.
- Avoid smoking—even socially! Studies suggest that smoking damages the elastin and collagen fibres found in the skin, making it less firm and resilient. And the constant puckering of the lips and squinting from smoking causes wrinkles around the lips and eyes too. Smoking also

makes the skin sallow and grey in appearance because it inhibits your circulation, thus depriving your skin cells of oxygen. Saggy, grey, wrinkly skin is not glamorous at all!

- Maintain your fitness. Yes with age, excess weight can accumulate under the chin, the neck or cheeks, giving the skin an older look—and no Glama puss wants to look like a turkey! A balanced diet, drinking plenty of water and exercise can greatly improve the appearance of the skin. Improved muscle tone and circulation also help to keep the skin looking young.

- Smile! Your face tends to adapt to the expressions you carry most of the time. If you often frown or scowl, your skin is more likely to develop lines or wrinkles between the eyes, down-turning lines at the corners of the mouth, and other lines or furrows that mark a frowning facial expression. A smiling, relaxed expression will help keep you looking younger.

- Sleeping on your face can cause sleep wrinkles. Believe it or not, sleeping in the same position most of the night for years can permanently crease your skin. With a small pillow under the lower spine, it is possible to sleep on your back comfortably without causing wrinkles on your face. On the flip side, you do need sufficient sleep to keep your skin looking vibrant—it is during these hours that your skin repairs itself. Lack of sleep can lead to dull-looking skin and puffy eyes with dark rings underneath them. Yuck! So make sure you get between seven and nine hours of blissful sleep each night. You know what they say—every Glama gal needs her beauty sleep!

Make-up the Face You Show the World

Did you know that the philosophers and mystics of Ancient Greece invented the root word for cosmetics—'cosmos'? They probably wore quite a bit of them too! Cosmetics have been worn by Glama women for centuries. Archeologists have uncovered the earliest remnants of make-up in Egypt, dating back to the 4th millennium BC. They found eye make-up and ornate objects used to apply perfumed lotions and soothing skin balms.

Greek women applied chalk to their faces to attract attention, Egyptian women wore foundation to protect their skin from the hot sun and black kohl around their eyes, and Persian women used henna to dye their hair. Women of the Italian Renaissance used lead paint as a face whitener, while in 18th century France, red rouge and lipstick became all the rage. The Victorian face of minimal make-up was in fashion right up until the twenties, when glamour really came to the fore. Red lipstick became a social necessity. From the thirties to the fifties, make-up was the epitome of glamour, with the looks of various Hollywood stars the vogue, while the sixties brought about dark-rimmed eyes and white lipstick. Today's make-up is a mixture of past styles with an emphasis on the natural look—a look that took centuries of glamour to achieve.

A cleverly made-up face, using Glama skill, is crucial when stepping out the door into the world. Whether you're going to the office, a flash dinner party, a girls' lunch at a chic cafe, a movie premiere, or just window shopping, show your cosmetic flair with the perfect make-up—here's how.

Foundation

All faces have either a pink or yellow base to the skin tone, so you need to work out which base you have before you find the right foundation. Simple? Yes! Look at the colour of your nail bed or pinch the skin under your arm. Does the tone appear more reddish-orange, reddish-blue, pinkish-blue, peachy or yellowish? Once you determine this, you'll have a benchmark for your natural tone and can find your perfect foundation.

It's best to apply foundation with a slightly damp make-up sponge for a more even application. Liquid foundations are the best for a dewy, fresh look because they come in oil-free, water-based or moisturising blends. Whipped or creme foundations are great for medium to high coverage and are usually better for dry, mature skins too. Pancake and make-up sticks give the most complete coverage of all and are good for ruddy complexions that need more protection from the sun or wind.

Remember to pick a foundation that blends invisibly into the skin on your neck. If you have to put foundation on your neck and decolletage, check that it isn't too dark, too pink or too orange a pigment. In fact, the best place to test the right colour for your foundation, when purchasing some, is on the lower chin and neck area—not on your wrist (your hands and arms are not always the same colour as your face and neck). Leave the foundation on, walk around the store for fifteen minutes and come back and see if it has changed colour through oxidation. If it looks invisible, then that's the one for you. If you've got an orange mark that looks like someone has been trying to choke you, go to another counter. And by the way, if you're a fair-skinned beauty and are worried about looking too pale (even if you've done all the tests and the foundation has come up trumps), don't make the mistake of letting the beauty consultant talk you into buying the darker tone for 'colour.' It's much more appealing and natural when you use your perfect skin-toned foundation all over your face. Colour can be added later with a sunny blush and some liquid bronzer over your cheeks and a light touch on your forehead and chin—in the places where a warm flush or touch of sun would show up naturally. And remember, most cosmetic companies make foundation with built-in sun-screens, so select a brand with the right level of protection for your skin.

If you need to use concealer, apply it under the eyes and to any skin discoloration or redness before you put on your foundation. For dark shadows under the eyes, use a liquid concealer lighter than your foundation—the best one for you is the one ever-so-slightly lighter than your skin tone. Always use a lightweight, creamy or liquid concealer under your eyes. Avoid concealer sticks as they tend to pull the delicate skin around too much. Save these for hiding spots, freckles or pimples on the rest of the face.

Eyeliner

Look in the mirror and study the shape, size and colour of your eyes. Are they round or oval, or shaped like an almond, walnut or lemon? Are your eyes wide, long, small or deep set? Are they blue, green, brown or hazel in colour? Learning the right application and tricks to accentuate the shape, size and colour of your eyes is essential for perfect eye make-up—this is only achieved through trial and error though (or by consulting a make-up artist). For example, if you have small eyes, don't line all the way around the eye—this makes them even smaller. Draw the eyeliner on the outer corners of the top lid only, and underneath just draw about halfway to get some definition. For deep set eyes, try coloured eyeliners as black tends to push the eye back even further. Apply a paler shade to the lid to open up the eye and the same colour or a slightly darker eye shadow in the crease. Following is our Glama guide for expert eyeliner application:

1. Draw a line close to the base of your eyelashes with the eyeliner. Whether you use pencil or a liquid liner, a steady hand and lots of practice is needed to perfect a beautiful, fine line. A good trick is to hold your head back so you can look down into the mirror. It makes it easier to apply the liner.

2. If you are using liquid or cake eyeliner and water, blot the eyeliner brush with a tissue to remove any excess fluid. Hold the eyelid skin taut and, starting from the inner corner of the eye, rest the brush or pencil on top of the lashes. Next sweep the brush gently along the upper lids, keeping close to the base of your lashes, maintaining one continuous line to the outer corner. For daytime make-up, don't extend the eyeliner, but for night-time or for more Glama eyes, extend upwards and outwards for a retro flip. For a darker and stronger line, leave the liner to dry for twenty seconds and then go back over the line. Some eyeliner styles are left untouched, flipped up on the edges and sharp, while other rounder, smoky-lined eyes involve smudging with a sponge applicator to soften the edges. Whichever Glama style you choose is up to you.

3. To allow the liner to set completely and avoid smearing later, brush the liner over with a matching black or dark brown/navy powdered eye shadow applied with a small pointed brush.

4. For the lower lashes it's best to use an eyeliner pencil in the matching colour instead of liquid liner—this looks less harsh. Run the pencil along the bottom outer rim of the eye, close to the base of the lashes, drawing it right into the inner corner. It needs to be extremely fine and can be applied to the outer lower corners to open and accentuate the eyes if you wish.

5. Finally, soften the lower line by smudging it with a cotton bud or pointed sponge applicator. Don't smudge or spread it out too much unless you want that panda bear look and you're are under 25!

For Glamazons with heavy or overhanging eyelids (consider an eye job, but if that's impossible then...) never ever use frosted or shimmery eye make-up right on the heavy area or overhanging crease. Actually no woman over forty should wear shimmery, glittery make-up all over the eye because it accentuates lines and loose skin. You may apply a little on the eyelid and a tiny touch right under the outer brow if you must, but only ever put a matt shadow along the socket area. Don't use any kind of pastel colours such as blue, purples or greens—these will only emphasise the problem. Stick with medium browns or matt greys along the crease line to help set back the eyes.

If you have blue, green or light eyes, don't overdo the black and dark eye make-up—it can be too heavy and dull for you. Try out some of the coloured eyeliners and mascaras on the market, which still define the eye but don't overdo it. Dark violets, navy and deep green colours look beautiful on lighter eyes.

If you have brown or black eyes, avoid bright blues and pastel pinks, especially inside the crease of the eye. Some blue or green pastel colours can be applied on the eyelid, but you still need definition with darker tones to balance the make-up with your dark exotic eyes. When using blues or pastels always apply a dark grey or navy powder in the crease of your eye and a black or navy pencil or blended liquid liner to finish the look.

Eye Shadow

Eye shadow can make you look the right vixen in the Glama stakes—you just need to know how to apply it correctly. First, decide if you're going for a day, night or full-on party Glama look and choose your colours accordingly. Second, define your eye shape (almond, round, narrow) and size. Do you have a large or small lid area with a clearly defined crease? Or is it flat with no marked crease? Once you've determined your eye shape and size, flick through a few beauty magazines and study models whose eye shape is similar to yours and critique their style—this way you'll have ideas to work from. Once you have established all this, you can start applying your Glama shadow.

Always apply eye shadow with either an applicator or an angled brush. For long lasting and smear proof eyes, use translucent or colour-free powder first over the entire upper eye area, then use a powdered eye shadow to add colour and emphasis. Powdered eye shadow stays put much longer than the cream-based ones.

The general rule to eye shadow application, whatever the colour combination used, is to swipe a lighter colour directly onto the eyelid and then a darker one above into the crease. Then blend both edges together with the brush or applicator. There are exceptions to that rule, but every eye shape suits that particular combination. Start with a small amount, and then build up the colour if needed. If you want more definition or a Glama evening look then black, brown or navy liquid eyeliner is the best definer to use with eye shadow.

Mascara

Mascara is magnificent—it really is so versatile. For a natural look apply one coat, for a dramatic look apply two coats, and for a smouldering look apply three. Always start with one coat and build the layers until you get the look you want. If you want really curly lashes, start by curling your lashes with an eyelash curler to open the eye area.

To apply perfect mascara, hold the wand horizontally and sweep the mascara from the roots to the ends, rolling the wand slightly as you move through the lashes—this will make them look really lush and thick. Then comb through the lashes using an eyelash brush or a clean mascara wand to prevent clogging and to keep the lashes separated. Finally, apply mascara to the lower lashes, but only on the outer edges.

Beautiful Brows

Grab a magnifying mirror and find some good light to produce the perfect face-framers! Keeping your eyebrows regularly groomed and plucked caps off the ultimate Glama make-up—day or night. A beautiful brow shape is achieved when the brow line begins slightly thicker from the inner corner of your eye, peaking up and getting gradually slimmer as it reaches the natural high point of your brow. As the brow slants downwards, allow it to get thinner as it stretches back towards the outer corners of your eye.

There is an easy way to make the brow look in proportion to your face. Lay a pencil from the base of your nose to the outer corner of your eye—the point where the pencil meets the brow is where your brow should finish. Mark the spot with a dab of eyeliner if you wish. Then place the pencil along the side of your nose to line up the inside point of your brow with the inside corner of each eye—that's the point of no return for plucking so go no further back or forward than that. A rule of thumb is that the highest point of the arch of your brow should line up with the outside edge of your pupil. You can mark that too if you want. Soon all this will become second nature and your brows will start to grow into that shape.

The best time to pluck your eyebrows is after bathing—the heat from the steam allows the hair to pull out more easily. Always pluck from underneath your eyebrow and remove the hairs in the same direction as they grow. While in the process of plucking, keep checking to see that you aren't removing too many hairs in one area. An ice cube will quickly solve any redness once you have finished.

To give your eyebrows extra definition, use an eyebrow pencil that matches their natural colour. Lightly draw the colour over your brows—but not too dark—you don't want them to look like they've been glued on.

The Paris Pout—Lippy Do's

To pull off the perfect blot lipstick, pull apart a two-ply tissue and blot your mouth. Apply foundation or concealer to your lips at the same time as you make-up the rest of your face. Next outline your lips with a slightly darker lip pencil than your chosen lipstick to give a clean edge and the illusion of fatter lips. Apply your lipstick generously over your entire lips and then blot with the tissue—it's best to put on your lipstick with a brush for a perfect application. Next take a still paler version of your lipstick, for example, for a purple-red lipstick, try pink; or for an orange-red, try peach and so on. With a lip brush dot the paler lipstick just on the centre of your lower lip (and a little on the centre of the top lip if your mouth needs the balance). For the party girl, night Glama effect, add an extra touch of shimmery lip gloss or bronzer.

The best way to make your teeth look white is to wear red lipstick. Even a reddish-brown colour rather than an orange-brown will show off the whiteness of your smile.

These days, many lipsticks have built-in conditioners, which help keep your lips soft and moist. So check that the lipstick contains this when buying a new colour.

Beautiful Blush

To avoid overdoing blush and looking like a clown, try to apply blusher near a sunlit window or under medium level electric light. A secret trick models use is to apply lipstick first—this will tell you if you actually need any blush that day and, if so, how much. Don't stand too close to the mirror—take a few steps back and wear your glasses if you have to! Smile to bring out the natural contours of your cheeks and swoosh a soft sweep of colour across the apple of your cheek. The old fashioned 'suck your cheeks in and apply in the sink holes' is a big no-no. Never use coloured blush as a face definer or to try and slim down your face. Blush is purely for a soft accent of healthy colour. A subtle sweep of the right coloured blush can lift up your cheekbones and enhance your bone structure right away, but beware, the edges of the colour to your skin should be so subtle that they are not seen at all.

Powder blush should be applied after foundation or set with powder. Apply cream or liquid blusher only on top of powder-free foundation or bare skin. Blusher should be carefully blended and the right shade for you will enhance your glow while the wrong one quickly drains natural health and colour away from your face. For very pale skin, the softest pastel pinks are the best (avoid all the brown tones). Fair to medium skin best suits pastel pinks, peaches, and light sandy terracottas in summer (avoid purples or you'll look bruised). Olive skin suits pink, rose tones and pinkish-brown bronzers (avoid all orange-yellow tones and gold bronzers. Pink and silvery shimmers are OK though). Oriental skin works best with soft pinks, pastel rose, pale plums and terracotta tones in summer, but not orange or yellow tones (silvery shine highlighters look gorgeous however). Black skin suits light to deep plum hues, deep to lighter rose (depending entirely on the hue of the skin), and gold highlighters and deep orange-bronze shimmers look fantastic.

A good brush is essential for powder blush application, while a clean triangle sponge is best for liquid or cream blush. So as not to overload the brush, sweep it across a tissue before applying to your face. Apply the blush in the same direction as the hair on your face (downward) to give a clean finish.

So, cast away phrases such as 'middle aged' and 'old' because with the right make-up, a Glamazon will shine at any age. And remember, in the world of Glama there's just 'birth' and then one big, fabulous life.

'There are
no ugly women,
only lazy ones.'

Helena Rubinstein

Chapter Ten

SECRETS, LIES AND GAFFER TAPE

'Age shall not wither her nor the years condemn!' And like Cleopatra, a Glamazon will use all her assets and do whatever is needed to achieve her goals and always look her stunning best. The fountain of youth may be a legend, but nowadays the lure of eternal beauty is close to becoming a reality. Yes, alongside her treasured photo of the Dalai Lama, the Glamazon has another picture—her guru of beauty, her cosmetic surgeon.

Four Steps to Help Ensure a Successful Outcome

If you are considering cosmetic enhancement then there are atleast four important steps you need to undertake to ensure you receive proper professional work. You don't want to end up looking like you've spent a week in a wind tunnel or have just gone twenty rounds in the ring with Mohammed Ali. You should also keep in mind that the desired result of any plastic surgery is an improvement, not perfection.

Step 1. Finding a Surgeon

In selecting a surgeon, your first challenge is to develop a list of candidates. It's really important for you to understand that not all medical practitioners that perform cosmetic surgery are plastic surgeons, or even practitioners with formal surgical qualifications. So, how do you find a good plastic or cosmetic surgeon?

Look to your friends. Talk to someone who has undergone a procedure like the one you are considering. However, as every patient's needs are unique, you can't assume their surgeon will be right for you.

Speak to your family doctor or other surgical specialists. For example, an otolaryngologist (ENT) or a cardiologist may be able to give you a good referral. If so, ask them if they have referred patients previously and whether they obtained positive feedback from those patients. Your GP can provide you with referrals to each of your surgeons. Without a referral you may not obtain a Medicare rebate, should one be available for your procedure.

Call a hospital of your choice and ask for the names of certified surgeons with hospital privileges who perform the procedure you are considering.

The Australian Society of Plastic Surgeons (ASPS) can give you advice and post you a list of your state's members. ASPS members are all fully qualified in both reconstructive and cosmetic surgery. All members are fellows of the Royal Australasian College of Surgeons (FRACS), the benchmark standard for surgical training within Australia, or its equivalent. Each surgeon has a record of accomplishment in their field and a commitment to high ethical standards.

Your local *Yellow Pages* is a convenient reference source as well. Look under 'medical practitioners' to locate a surgeon (FRACS) in your area. Your local newspaper may also be a source of information.

Media interviews or stories involving surgeons are not testimonies to their credentials and experience and is sometimes paid advertising by the surgeon. So don't believe everything you read in the magazines or see on television about the work performed and always check the certification of any surgeon you are considering using.

Step 2. Credentials Check

Now that you have compiled a list of cosmetic surgeons, you need to thoroughly check their qualifications and credentials. Most surgeons have letters that appear after their names, so check whether they are relevant to your intended procedure. Credentials do not guarantee a positive outcome, but they can significantly increase the odds of success. By contacting hospitals, professional societies such as the ASPS and the surgeon's office, you can obtain the following important information:

- What initial training did the surgeon undergo?
- In which specialty area did they train? Rhinoplasty? Laser resurfacing?
- How many years did they train?
- How comprehensive was their training?
- How relevant is their training to cosmetic surgery?

Most surgeons in Australia are certified by the Royal Australasian College of Surgeons—the letters 'FRACS' should appear in your surgeon's credentials. The letters after your surgeon's name may also indicate membership of a professional society. It is important to check on the legitimacy of the organisation or practice and whether your surgeon is a member in good standing. For international associations, the Internet can be a useful resource.

Not all surgeons have hospital privileges. Make sure the procedure you wish to undergo will be performed in either a private hospital or a day procedure centre registered with the state health department or accredited by the Australian Council on Health Care Standards or a similar organisation.

Has the surgeon had experience of the specific procedure you require? Some procedures may be new and their experience necessarily less. A fully trained plastic surgeon will easily bring skills to a new procedure, which is often only a progression of an established one.

Step 3. Initial Consultation

Once you have a shortlist of two or three surgeons, you may wish to have an initial consultation with each of them. By doing so, you can obtain their opinions on the type of surgery you require, their fees, their responses to your questions and how they explain the risks associated with your procedure. Bear in mind that consultations will most likely attract a fee regardless of whether you choose the surgeon to operate on you or not.

When undergoing a consultation, the surgeon should welcome any questions you may have concerning your procedure including answering any queries about their training and credentials, their experience and personal techniques, their fees and payment policies and so on. Prepare your list of questions in order to easily assess and compare each surgeon's response. Don't forget to make notes. If you don't understand something, ask the question again. A surgeon should speak to you in language you can understand.

Your surgeon should also interview you with questions and issues regarding:

- Your motivation and expectations for the procedure, if the surgeon believes these to be relevant.
- Alternatives, if appropriate, without pressuring you into procedures you may not want.
- The risks and variations in outcome for your procedure. Before and after images may be introduced at this point.
- Your comments and/or concerns regarding the surgeon's recommendation.
- The surgeon should not rush you into making a decision. You should be

encouraged to wait at least a week before scheduling your surgical procedure. This 'cooling off' period is vital. A second consultation is commonly arranged and is recommended.

Step 4. Your Decision

Now that you've done your homework and met with the surgeons personally, selection from your shortlist should be fairly easy. If you are still uncertain whether you should proceed with cosmetic surgery, then perhaps you should re-examine your expectations of cosmetic surgery and be honest with yourself. It is vital that you are psychologically prepared to undergo the procedure. Emotional stability is the primary factor to be considered before undergoing any aesthetic surgery.

Plastic Surgery— the Common Procedures

Once you have considered all the pros and cons of plastic surgery and are happy with all the possible outcomes, then book your operation. There are many types of plastic surgery you can consider to improve your appearance.

Liposuction

Suction-assisted lipectomy is an aesthetic (cosmetic) surgical procedure designed to remove localised collections of fat, such as those that occur on the thighs, buttocks and abdomen, as well as on the arms, neck and under the chin. Suction lipectomy may be used to improve your overall body appearance by reducing and recontouring localised collections of fat.

A consultation with your plastic surgeon is the first step to considering a suction lipectomy. You should frankly discuss your goals and expectations, and your plastic surgeon will explain to you whether this operation is right for you.

Before undergoing suction lipectomy, it is important to understand that a 'new body' does not guarantee a new life or an end to all your personal problems. It is mostly the mental attitude of the individual that determines a successful outcome. Suction lipectomy may be ideal for patients who have bulges that persist after diet and exercise, but it is not a substitute for weight loss, nor a cure for obesity.

Laser Resurfacing

Essentially, lasers are machines that emit very pure forms of light. There are specific lasers for brown spots, hair removal, and resurfacing of the skin. The skin resurfacing lasers most commonly used by plastic surgeons are the carbon dioxide (CO_2) and erbium lasers. Laser treatments may be recommended to you for problems such as:

- The effects of age, sun exposure, acne and smoking.
- Wrinkles around the eyes, lips, cheeks and forehead.
- Permanent blemishes and uneven skin.
- Freckles and liver spots.
- Hyper pigmentation (increased pigmentation).
- Acne and pitted or chicken pox scars.
- Superficial scars.
- Raised benign skin lesions.
- Sagging eyelids.

When laser resurfacing is carried out by a qualified, experienced plastic surgeon, complications are infrequent and then, usually minor. However, because individuals vary greatly in their anatomy, physical reactions and healing abilities, an outcome is never completely predictable. And you will be more sensitive to the rays of the sun and must use a sunscreen (at least SPF15[+]) when outdoors. Therefore, if you are planning to undergo laser restructuring, it is important to see a well-trained and competent plastic surgeon for advice and treatment because it takes a careful hand and experience to administer this treatment effectively.

Augmentation Mammoplasty

Augmentation mammoplasty is an aesthetic (cosmetic) surgical procedure to increase the size of breasts. Augmentation mammoplasty will also correct slight sagging of the breast and can increase breast firmness. A similar procedure can be used to recreate a breast after a mastectomy. You may wish to have an augmentation mammoplasty if you feel your breasts are smaller than normal or out of proportion to your body size. Augmentation mammoplasty is also useful if your breasts are unequal in size or if they have decreased in size following pregnancy.

There are currently several techniques for augmentation mammoplasty, but they all involve the insertion of a saline-filled (salt water) implant or a silicone gel implant either behind the breast tissue or behind the pectoral muscle. The implant is inserted through a small incision either under the breast, around the nipple or in the armpit. Your plastic surgeon will determine which approach would be most appropriate for you. But it is important to note that there is a lot of documented problems associated with silicone gel implants. So do your research.

The goal of your surgery is to augment your breasts to a size that is in better proportion with your physique. Often a B–C cup size is obtained. Your surgeon is the best person to determine whether your expectations are achievable.

Facelift

A facelift is an aesthetic (cosmetic) surgical procedure to improve and sometimes eliminate evidence of ageing on the face and neck. A consultation with a qualified plastic surgeon is the first step when you are considering a facelift. It is important to consider that a 'new face' does not guarantee a new life or an end to all your personal problems.

Your desire might be to have a facelift to correct signs of ageing such as lines and wrinkles, sagging facial skin or a 'turkey gobbler' neck. But remember that a facelift, even a 'mini lift,' or a so-called 'half face,' is major surgery and shouldn't be taken lightly. Apart from discussing with your surgeon any side effects he or she may anticipate, it is also wise to talk over your decision with your long term partner or husband. A facelift is not something you can just hide away from your partner with, 'I'm just going away for the weekend with a couple of girl-friends!' After you check out of hospital, you'll need at least one week of after care (preferably away from your lover at a friend's place or at a private hospital), by a very good Glama buddy, nurse or relative. And even after you come back home, he will notice some leftover swelling and bruising.

And of course, there are other less invasive treatments such as botox, collagen and Restalyn injections that can serve as a preventive to ageing as well.

But whatever you choose to have, any kind of cosmetic surgery should be well thought out with the knowledge that you can improve your appearance, but your Glama attitude and inner allure is entirely up to you.

'The great thing about plastic surgery... is that you can have absolutely everything, but admit to absolutely nothing.'

Reportedly etched on Nefertiti's make-up box

Chapter Eleven

GLAMA BY THE STARS

Can you choose your soulmate by the stars? And what is it within all of us that prompts us to choose certain clothing, hair and trends? Frequently our relationship choices, our style of dress, fashion accessories, attitudes and personal preferences originate from the influence of our star sign. As a style example, frequently the earth signs—Taurus, Virgo and Capricorn—even in urban conditions, adopt a casual, elegant look that makes them appear as if they are poised to head for the country. More conservative in nature, they tend to be neat and tidy and less dramatic in their appearance than other signs.

Fire signs—Aries, Leo and Sagittarius—are the bold and daring fashionistas of the zodiac. They dress with a flair for a more 'showbiz' or dramatic appearance. Because of their wilful and feisty natures, they tend to be slightly reckless about what they wear and can be extreme or overstated in their mode of dress. Although fire signs are often fashion risk-takers and style-setters, many of them still magically appear immaculate most of the time. These signs (when they have reason to) can put a lot of input into their 'costumes' or styling. That's why many a fire-sign Glamazon has influenced fashion trends in a big way—look at Leos Jackie Kennedy Onassis, Madonna and Jennifer Lopez.

The Air signs—Gemini, Libra and Aquarius—inherently have a touch of fashion mystery surrounding them. They naturally appear to have Glama and their zodiac influence of being airily creative can make them fashion and clothing chameleons. They can also be outrageously put together or fashionably unkempt. They are the signs most likely to have body art, such as piercing and tattoos in extreme cases.

Lastly the mysterious water signs—Cancer, Scorpio and Pisces—belong to the zodiac sign group that presents the greatest ideas when it comes to fashion imagination. They express their imaginative, dream-like approach to life in their unique self-expression, emotional displays, multi-talents and often in their flamboyant, dramatic appearance (and matching behaviour). Their moods often shape their appearance and their clothes can become more like costumes than everyday wear. You'll often discover with the water sign Glamazon that she is either dressed up to the nines or getting around in grunge (she's an all-or-nothing kind of dresser).

Now looking through the window that astrology provides to each zodiac sign, let's examine how each is likely to influence a Glamazon's fashion trends and general personal style and let's not forget, how to choose our perfect Glama man.

The Aries Glamazon

Ruled by Mars, the male energy planet, it's no wonder this star gal of the zodiac often feels more comfortable wearing trousers than dresses. She is the tomboy of the zodiac and this is reflected in her fashion style. The masculine energy planet, Mars, makes her a strong feminine force to reckon with. She's feisty, independent and strong-willed, and when it comes to making a fashion statement she strikes a dramatic presence. This Glamazon can be the more outrageous of the zodiac star girls and she can pack a powerful social, fashion and success punch. Renowned for being the most impatient gal of the zodiac, the Aries Glamazon usually dislikes anything or anyone (particularly fashion accessories or clothing) that slows her down. She's the gal in a hurry and she doesn't have time to dilly-dally or mess around with trivia.

Tempestuous and daring, the Aries Glamazon often selects a personal style or fashion look that stands out in the crowd. She also has a preference for clothes that are easy to wear and require easy maintenance. Surprisingly, she can be comfortable running around in the highest of all stilettos—the type that would have other less hardy gals wilting as they think of nothing else but eventually taking off these trapeze artist shoes and opting for a good foot massage or soak.

When it comes to shopping indulgences, the Aries Glamazon often goes on shopping binges and buys the most peculiar bits and pieces. As it is usually tedious for her to stop long enough to try things on, the Aries Glamazon often purchases items that need to be returned. It irritates her to fiddle with lots of buttons, buckle up shoes, or arrange fancy bows. Consequently, if she purchases items that have fiddly requirements, they usually sit in her closet unworn. Unless she wants something for a very special occasion, she prefers easy clothes that she can quickly slip in or out of, or put on and pull off. Passionate in nature (because her ruler Mars governs lust and passion), the Aries Glamazon usually dresses in fashions that boldly promote her sexual charms. She can be quite a sexual siren and this is frequently represented in her style of dress, which can be extremely seductive (especially when she's on a man hunt).

Aries

Basic fashion style

'Hey, look at me!' outfits. The Aries Glamazon loves bold and daring clothes.

Best fashion colour

Red and other bright colours.

Best fashion shoe

Dangerously high stilettos or workman's clumpy boots.

Must-have make-up item

Black eyeliner for added eye-flashing drama.

Hair

Windswept and Glama-cut.

Hemline

Whatever hemline is the most daring and likely to raise eyebrows.

Can't-live-without fashion accessory

A full-to-the-brim Gucci handbag.

Shopping habits

The Aries Glamazon is highly impulsive when she shops, which is why she often races in and buys things she never ends up wearing or using.

Aries fashion icons

Sarah Jessica Parker, Elle MacPherson, Mariah Carey, Diana Ross, Paloma Picasso, Kate Hudson and Celine Dion.

The Taurus Glamazon

Ruled by the pleasure-oriented and overly indulgent planet, Venus, Taurus Glamazons have an inner compass that sets itself at birth towards finding the best shops. Nobody can match a Taurus Glamazon when it comes to indulging in a good dose of retail therapy. In the shopping and accumulation of possessions stakes, she can set a dedicated standard that other signs of the zodiac find impossible to beat. There is no shopper on the planet as committed as a Taurus shopper, when she's in shopping mode.

Because she is ruled by the fashionista guru planet, Venus, looking good, having fun, admiring beauty, seeking out pleasure and sensuality all mean a great deal to her. Fortunately for the Taurus Glamazon, because she is born to shop, she usually gets the shopper's equivalent of a black belt. Plus with Venus ruling her, the benefits of having charm and inner and outer beauty are usually part of her zodiac sign's blessing. There is many a Taurus beauty on this planet and they were naturally born that way.

Being a nature lover, this connection to the earth and its fauna and flora can influence her fashion trends and choice of colour. The Taurus Glamazon will love wearing her 'dressed down' clothes that are suitable for country homes or ranches. She innately knows that you cannot beat nature's colour scheme and she understands how to fit herself glamorously into nature's scenery and add to it with her personal take on fashion. She always looks fabulous in riding pants, safari outfits and biker jackets. The Taurus Glamazon is frequently found working in show business, health, beauty and fashion arenas. Being an earth sign, she usually has a businesslike attitude to life and an organised approach to keeping her life and looks in good order. She can suffer from weight problems because Venus makes her a lover of good food and wine.

The Taurus Glamazon invests in good quality, classic clothes, rather than flippant fashion trends. She is unlikely to have piercing or sport tattoos. If she is strongly influenced by her star sign, she prefers to dress in simple upmarket fashion rather than grunge or anything that is jarring to the eye. If you see an outrageously 'eye-dazzling' or tattooed Taurus Glamazon, she usually has a 'special reason' for adopting such a wild at heart appearance. She can even be a rock and roll star like Taurus Glamazon, Cher.

If their budget can afford it, a true Taurus Glamazon can become an ardent art collector, fashion follower and leader, or an interior design trendsetter. But the Taurus Glamazon has some personal trials to overcome. Due to her Venus-inspired inclination to overindulge, the Taurus Glamazon needs to place herself on perpetual diets, as the temptations of a sweet tooth and second helpings usually are a strong part of her nature.

Taurus

Basic fashion style
Striking but conservative (even if she is a fashionista).

Best fashion colour
Pinks and blues.

Best fashion shoe
Slingbacks.

Must-have make-up item
The right lip gloss.

Hair
She goes for a great cut, style and highlights. She messes with her hair a lot and often messes up!

Hemline
Longish.

Can't-live-without fashion accessory
A sturdy Prada bag (of ample size, of course!).

Shopping habits
She's a compulsive shopper. She'll shop for everything and anything and she's also very self-indulgent. When she sees anything at all that catches her eye, she finds it hard to resist, whether she needs it or not.

Taurus fashion icons
Cate Blanchett, Michelle Pfeiffer, Bianca Jagger, Barbra Streisand, Cher, Andie McDowell, Janet Jackson, Uma Thurman and Audrey Hepburn.

The Gemini Glamazon

Ruled by the planet of quick-thinking and communication, Mercury, the Gemini Glamazon's personal style can be dazzling! When she is in top fashion form, the way she puts together a look is often envied (and copied) by others. The Gemini Glamazon is naturally a style leader for many different reasons, but mainly her fashion talent comes from the updated, original, quirky and unique way of packageing and presenting herself. Because she thinks differently from most other people, she doesn't need to do too much to stand out in any crowd. She has a natural ability to turn heads or come across 'as someone who looks interesting.'

Often born with a different look from the average looking gal, if she doesn't have this 'fashion or physical difference' as her birthright, she has sufficient creativity and vision to create this uniqueness for herself. Not naturally a follower of fashion, she prefers to look different, and that's why she chooses unusual looks or styles over those that everyone else is adopting. As a result, she doesn't get stuck in any fashion ruts. The Gemini Glamazon can change looks or styles in an instant. In fact, she loves to move into a totally different style or make a different fashion statement from the one she had yesterday—and she often does this in a dramatic way. This fashion inventiveness means that she is often involved in design, fashion, modelling, acting or other pursuits that can lead to fame or fortune. She may also be involved or employed in the media, or in fields that involve art, decoration or photography. What helps her throughout her life is her ability to exist in a league of her own when it comes to the way she chooses her star style. It helps her in the fashion stakes that she has an innate youthful quality (part of the Gemini make-up), that she manages to maintain even into older age.

Because of the twin symbol that depicts her sign, a Gemini Glamazon has the ability to be very adaptable and portray the role of total opposites. Being an extremist, she can outwardly mirror the two twin sides of her character by the clothes or attitudes she adopts. For example, her moods can move rapidly between the optimist and the pessimist and this mood swing can impact on the colours and styles she wears. Many times she can become deeply infatuated with a fashion style, a person or situation, and then turn around and become totally disillusioned about the same situation over a short space of time.

Being the twin sign also propels the Gemini gal through uncertainty and anxiety when shopping or choosing what to wear. She'll put on an outfit, then take it off and replace it with another. Or she'll wear an outfit and think the whole time she is wearing it, 'I should have worn something else!' Because her mind clicks over at super-rapid speed, this gal is a natural worrywart. She'll not only get herself keyed up about what to wear or buy, but she has a tendency to worry about money, relationships, general well-being, health, fitness and even the weather. Because of her ever-changing mind, the Gemini Glamazon can experience tremendous weight fluctuations throughout her lifetime. You can find the thinnest of thin Geminis (she is prone to illnesses like anorexia nervosa), and the obese Gemini, as her twin-minded energy brings her metabolism into conflict when her emotions go awry.

Gemini

Basic fashion style

She's a fashion chameleon. She can change her look in an instant and sometimes you would never even recognise her when she does.

Best fashion colour

Yellow and gold.

Best fashion shoe

Sexy open-toed stiletto sandal.

Must-have make-up item

The perfect brow pencil.

Hair

Sassy and funky—one that is original—and lots of different hair colours.

Hemline

The shorter the better.

Can't-live-without fashion accessory

The latest mobile phone.

Shopping habits

She's something of a shopping neurotic. She worries about shopping (more than simply enjoying it), and often suffers from shopper's remorse after she has gone and spent too much money.

Gemini fashion icons

Kylie Minogue, Naomi Campbell, Karen Mulder, Nicole Kidman, Brooke Shields, Jewel, Stevie Nicks, Elizabeth Hurley, Angelina Jolie and Marilyn Monroe.

The Cancer Glamazon

Ruled by the ever-changing Moon, the Cancer Glamazon is probably the most extreme girly-Glamazon of all the zodiac signs. She's either confident or lack-lustre...and her moods change erratically. On a bad day, she will hide away from the world, while on a good day she'll want to be noticed. She's a sensitive soul (even if at times she appears extremely tough on the outside), because this gal is born under the zodiac sign that aligns with the feminine principles. Consequently, she is ruled by her emotions. This connection to the feminine side of her personality not only gives her beauty and softness, plus abundant talent and imagination, but it also spins her into uncharted territory. She runs on a plethora of multi-dimensional moods, likes and dislikes, strengths and weaknesses, and personalities that swirl within her. Every day can tell a different story or bring about a different desire or fear for the Cancer Glamazon, that's why this gal has more than her fair share of bad hair days. The Cancer Glamazon (because of her mood and identity swings) feels a need to have many different fashion styles or outfits to fit in with her ever-changing moods and emotions. Check out her closet sometime—it is likely to be bulging with a wide variety of the best assortment of clothes—but when it comes to putting them together, most don't coordinate. Because she shops on a whim, this gal often finds herself with an abundance of outfits, but nothing to wear. She can collect dresses, bags, shoes and accessories but still end up not looking quite right or with mismatched accessories.

Because the Cancer Glamazon has such an active and vivid imagination, she is frequently swept away from reality by her dreams and fantasies whilst shopping.

The Cancer Glamazon doesn't think clearly when she is making an important purchase. She bases her shopping on impulse, not on logic or practical thinking. Because the Cancer Glamazon often shops when she is experiencing inner tension, she may suddenly find herself with shoes that don't fit, clothes the wrong size or items in her closet that she can't believe she purchased.

Accessories mean a lot to the Cancer Glamazon and she often has a treasure trove of accessories that resemble a modern day Aladdin's Cave in items, opulence and colour. And when it comes to colour, this gal is very sensitive. Certain colours even depress her, so she needs to consider this when selecting her outfit for day or night wear. The incorrect selection of any outfit or colour can spoil her entire time.

More than any other sign, the Cancer Glamazon is influenced by what she wears, feels or senses. If she receives a bad haircut or the wrong hair colour, she can sink into a long-running depression. So what she feels, wears, fears or imagines and projects outwardly via her overall appearance, plays a big role in deciding which side she lands on when she walks down life's fine line between Glamazon success or failure.

Cancer

Basic fashion style

She's a fantasy style gal and her clothes represent the fantasy costumes she sees herself wearing in her many imaginative dreams and musings.

Best fashion colours

Silver (like the Moon that rules her sign), and all the rainbow shades. Black when she's sad (which is frequently).

Best fashion shoe

Glitter glam evening shoes (the type that would be great in a Cinderella fairytale).

Must-have make-up item

Eye kajal or dark eyeliner.

Hair
Ultra-feminine style.

Hemline
The sexiest hemline she can come up with for any outfit.

Can't-live-without fashion accessory
The right star man on her arm.

Shopping habits
The Cancer Glamazon shops when she's experiencing 'bad hair days.' When this gal over-shops or starts buying junk, you know she's undergoing an emotional meltdown.

Cancer fashion icons
Pamela Anderson (think of those boobs), Princess Diana (think of those moods), Courtney Love, Imelda Marcos, Nancy Reagan, Gina Lollobrigida, Carly Simon and Lisa Rinna.

The Leo Glamazon

Ruled by the shining Sun, the centre of the solar system, the Leo Glamazon is usually found radiating in the social spotlight. She craves attention and enjoys being the recipient of lots of adoring attention, and when she isn't in the spotlight, she is probably dreaming about being celebrated, famous and embarrassingly rich and indulgent, very soon. Fortunately, for her, confidence is something the Leo Glamazon is born with and that helps her move forward in leaps and bounds. She often leaves those less confident star gals standing in her cosmic dust, wondering how she out-shone them so easily. With an inborn sense of her own self-worth and confidence, and her natural ability to be a trailblazer, the Leo Glamazon, once she hits her stride, is unstoppable. She is prepared to take a chance, do whatever it takes, and go the distance to get what she wants. It is a most unwise individual who underestimates her personal power and ability to get ahead. Remember her symbol is the lioness after all!

Often a brilliant leader of fashion, the Leo Glamazon has the confidence to leap into situations and handle conditions or fame that most others just dream about.

Consequently her self-belief, daring and bold nature can propel her into unique opportunities. She can do anything with fashion because she claims it and makes it her own. Whatever style she assumes (and she will transform herself up the fashion ladder by coming up with a new stunning style, whenever the next step is required), she does it in her own special way. She is not a follower of fashion; she is a creator of it. She is tuned into her own self-importance and this gives her the ability to make a fashion statement that others quickly follow.

The Leo Glamazon tends to make a bold fashion statement rather than a meek one. She prefers to overstate rather than understate and she isn't afraid to wear tradition-breaking outfits to the most unusual or conservative of occasions. She won't allow others' opinions to undermine her own fashion judgment and she is happy to travel her own personal fashion pathway through life, if it means she is breaking out of the fashion mould. Many a Leo Glamazon has changed the history of fashion—look at Jackie Kennedy Onassis and Madonna as two significant fashion guru examples.

Leo

Basic fashion style
Bold and daring. This gal loves to make a memorable fashion statement. She focuses on creating the 'wow' effect.

Best fashion colour
Black, red, gold and bold.

Best fashion shoe
Stilettos, stilettos and more stilettos.

Must-have make-up item
Perfume.

Hair
Long so she can toss it around or cropped ultra-short. When it comes to her hair, she's a fashionista extremist.

Hemline
Whatever she thinks will shock others and attract the most attention.

The Virgo Glamazon

Many a beauteous gal has been born under the zodiac sign of Virgo. Indeed, some of the most perfect trendsetters and fashion beauties are born under this sign's domain. Ruled by Mercury, the planet of all-over-the-place mental energy, the Virgo Glamazon is a creative thinker, youthful in outlook with a quick eye for catching and observing fashion detail. Like a clock, her mind seldom stops ticking over and whatever is reeling around in there (whether she's happy, sad, worried or positive about the future), impacts on her physicality, her looks and her fashion decisions. Her state of mind can also dramatically impact on her weight. More than any other sign of the zodiac, the Virgo Glamazon's health, looks and creativity can teeter-totter back and forth when her life goes through change, unsettled times or other uncertainties. She is particularly vulnerable to the impact her romantic relationships have on her moods. If she's going through relationship fears or upsets she quickly loses her unique and wonderful Earth Goddess glow.

As her mind tends towards worrying, it is easy for her to experience internal conflicts and sleepless nights. When swings of fate and fortune occur in her life, her fashion sense and general appearance can run from raggedy to regal, depending on what she's going through. She can swing from the most elegant gal on the planet when she is happy, into someone that resembles a grungy bag lady when she is feeling betrayed by life or vulnerable. Her appearance can alter dramatically at the hint of an emotional or mental upset.

The Virgo Glamazon loves nature and nature loves her. To feel great, the Virgo Glamazon often needs to seek out peace, harmony and personal tranquillity, and she can do this by organising regular trips to the country. Her desire for harmony may encourage her to explore meditation, yoga, religion and to travel down new age and other spiritual paths. These other worldly or spiritual connections can also affect her physical appearance, demeanour and fashion style selection. To feel calm and comfortable is something most Virgo Glamazons desire, that's why she will be attracted towards clothes or a fashion style that radiates with gentleness, femininity and serenity. Though she has her 'party-on phases'—and at these times she may choose bold, daring and garish clothing—these party clothes are worn to create a theatrical affect, rather than as an expression of who she is or her personal preference. When it comes to colours, white can be a very soothing tone for the Virgo Glamazon to wear, with many Virgos finding that wearing two tones, such as black and white, fits well when it comes to expressing who they are and what they are feeling. Innately the Virgo Glamazon is on a subliminal quest for perfection, particularly perfection within herself. This quest is often depicted in the way she selects or sets up her lifestyle, career and appearance. Subtle, tasteful colours and delicate feminine blends of different tones or hues are her preference. She also loves to wrap herself in a sense of spirituality or mysticism. This combined with a natural, sexy, earthy undertone is usually a part of the way the Virgo Glamazon puts her fashion style package together. And when she gets the package right she is a total knockout!

Virgo

Basic fashion style

She's the earthy, sensual, fashion goddess of the zodiac.

Best fashion colour

She looks wonderful in white and pastels.

Best fashion shoe

Delicate feminine styles or solid rock climbing hikers if she's an outdoorsy Virgo.

Must-have make-up item

Super strong sunscreen make-up to protect her delicate, fine skin.

Hair

Carefully and meticulously cut and styled in whatever look she's into at the moment.

Hemline

Edgy, suggestive and whimsical.

Can't-live-without fashion accessory

Magnifying make-up mirror.

Shopping habits

The Virgo Glamazon is usually a cautious shopper. Unless she's having a bad hair day and is going shopping for retail therapy she's likely to do her shopping research before she buys. The Virgo Glamazon likes to ensure that she is buying quality at a good price.

Virgo fashion icons

Claudia Schiffer, Sophia Loren, Cameron Diaz, Gloria Estafan, Shania Twain, Ingrid Bergman, Jacqueline Bisset and Faith Hill.

The Libra Glamazon

The Libra gal is a natural contender for becoming a fully fledged zodiac Glamazon. However, it is important to mention that there are two distinctively different types of Libra gals—those who were born when their ruling planet, the fashionista guru planet Venus was smiling, and those who were born when Venus was frowning. Those who were born when Venus was smiling are the zodiac's naturally beautiful and seductive Glamazons and they often become fashionistas of the highest levels. However, those born while Venus was frowning often get around in drudge clothing that resembles crinkled sheets off an unmade bed rather than a fashion garment. This type of Libran can also occasionally allow her body to go to pot, however, this section will focus on the Libra gal who was born while Venus was smiling (and, after all, they are likely to be the ones reading this anyway!).

The Libra Glamazon gal is blessed with being born with an eye for beauty. She is frequently the blessed receiver of glowing, natural beauty. She is usually talented too with good instincts for art, music, theatre and fashion. She is a natural hostess and these attributes can propel her to global social prominence (naturally her ruling planet, Venus, provides some lucky breaks and a helping hand in these areas!). She's smart too, and although she may not always set fashion trends herself, she knows how to adapt any style of fashion and claim it as her own. That's why you'll find so many Libra Glamazons clever at creating beauty and harmony in not just their personal style and appearance but also in the way their homes and environment are presented. When it comes to what she wears or the way she presents herself, the Libra Glamazon prefers to adopt a subtle fashion approach rather than a bulldozer, knock-them-down-in-the-aisles, one.

Although she appears delicate, her fragility can be misleading. The Libra Glamazon is much more resilient, powerful and adaptable than her feminine demeanour may suggest. She's also very sensual and knows the value of using her sensuality to her advantage. Sensuous and high-spirited, the Libra Glamazon is often extremely seductive and shrewd in the way she pursues her goals and sets about achieving her many missions in life. This gal can be highly ambitious. She may sometimes come across as a little-girl-lost, but rest assured, the Libra Glamazon usually knows exactly where she is going and knows exactly what she needs to do to get to her chosen destination. Never underestimate a Libra Glamazon—she's the fashionista with the punch of Rocky and the seductive beauty of Delilah combined!

Libra

Basic fashion style
 She manages to look subtly seductive without being sleazy.

Best fashion colour
 Violet and silver.

Best fashion shoe
 Boots (especially elegant ones).

Must-have make-up item

The perfect lipstick.

Hair

A healthy, feminine hairstyle (usually longer than short) in good condition.

Hemline

Saucy, but still modestly conservative.

Can't-live-without fashion accessory

The up-to-the-minute lingerie.

Shopping habits

She's wicked when it comes to shopping. This Glamazon girl can truly shop until she drops from exhaustion!

Libra fashion icons

Donna Karan, Heather Locklear, Catherine Zeta-Jones, Susan Sarandon, Toni Braxton, Serena Williams, Kate Winslet, Sarah Ferguson, Brigitte Bardot, Danni Minogue and Gwyneth Paltrow.

The Scorpio Glamazon

This Scorpio star gal can be the most creative fashion stylist and style-setter of the zodiac because she knows how to create a powerful impression and, best of all, she knows how to make the most of the looks she was given. Her special zodiac gift is that she knows how to make her own fashion statement. She can come up with her own 'look' that sets her apart from the crowd (and she does this frequently). She realises that clothes are part of the game of life and she dresses in order to enter into a role or social class. Consequently, the expression 'you can't judge a book by its cover', or for those into fashion, 'a gal by their choice of designer' best sums up the Scorpio gal more than any other. There is usually much more to a Scorpio Glamazon than meets the naked eye. She's a fashion work in progress and she's the one doing the work on herself...constantly!

Because she is such a strong individual, the Scorpio Glamazon dislikes imitating other people's fashion ideas. She prefers to come up with her own. Naturally a schemer, the Scorpio Glamazon usually has a few secret fashion ideas or plans for the future that she is keeping all to herself. She likes to surprise others by what she is wearing. Not only is she a person who likes to plan ahead with what she will wear next with extreme care, but she also has other nifty aspects to her powerful personality, such as being able to find bargains. Being a natural 'image creator' the Scorpio Glamazon's personal style is often not indicative at all of who she truly is. Her appearance can be carefully contrived, constructed, maintained and packaged. However, she is a creature of habit, so if this gal finds a look or fashion style that works for her and she feels comfortable with, she'll often keep that 'look' for her entire life.

The Scorpio Glamazon is usually envied by others. She has a wise head on her pretty shoulders and she is born with an innate knowingness about life and its requirements and games—that's why she has a knack for being in the right place at the right time, or meeting and connecting with the right people. Usually subtle in her way of dressing, her fashion message is sometimes more subliminally sexy than suggestive. The Scorpio Glamazon's ruling planet is Pluto, and in Greek mythology, Pluto was the Greek god who could put on his helmet and become invisible. Much the same applies to the Scorpio Glamazon. When she doesn't wish to be noticed or bothered she has the power to create an invisible barrier that allows her to pass by others unnoticed. The Scorpio Glamazon has the power to be noticed when she wants to be—this gives her a very mysterious illusiveness— a quality that no other zodiac sign can master. Consequently it isn't so much what the Scorpio Glamazon chooses to wear; it is more about the way she chooses to wear it that counts.

Fashion-wise the Scorpio Glamazon has very strong opinions about everything and this makes her more of a leader than a follower. She respects her own judgment or sense of what works and doesn't work for her when it comes to fashion. It is only rarely that she will rely on other people's fashion advice or counsel. The Scorpio Glamazon uses clothes as a stage prop and she has the ability to wear them so that they never overshadow her own special self. Her choice of clothes and fashion style are usually consistent and she doesn't vary them unless there's a very good reason. However, if she goes through a major life change, she can also alter her physical appearance (or fashion style) dramatically. It can sometimes seem as if she is assuming a new persona or adorning herself with the right fashion costume to move into the next act of the Glama play that is her life.

Scorpio

Basic fashion style
She wants to make a powerful fashion statement, not a meek one.

Best fashion colour
Black and darker shades.

Best fashion shoe
Manolo Blahnik shoes in any style.

Must-have make-up item
Black eye pencil.

Hair
She has her own unique style (something she creates which shows she has 'her own look').

Hemline
Whatever length suits her height and leg shape (she doesn't simply follow hemline fashion).

Can't-live-without fashion accessory
Her designer sunglasses.

Shopping habits
Freudian—if she is having lots of sex the Scorpio Glamazon will shop less than when she is living a more celibate existence.

Scorpio fashion icons
Meg Ryan, Demi Moore, Julia Roberts, Goldie Hawn, Maria Shriver, Hillary Rodham Clinton, Bo Derek, Jodie Foster, Grace Kelly and Lisa Bonet.

The Sagittarius Glamazon

Ruled by the philosophical, free-spirited planet of the zodiac, Jupiter, the Sagittarius Glamazon is regarded as a jetsetter; a high rolling gal. She's the one who loves to party and is usually ready, willing and able to actively seek out or create her next big adventure. You'll find her luxuriating in the high life all over the world in exotic locations or unusual places, mixing with the most bohemian or interesting of people. The fact that she is a thrillseeker at heart propels her at an early age towards the people and places that provide her with unique experiences. She has disdain for boredom and routine, and this desire to lead an exciting life can land her in hot water because she is also a risk-taker. Not too caught up in style, she still manages to have a fantastic fashion knack of creating her own look. The Sagittarius Glamazon usually doesn't follow other people's fashion trends, and she has a talent for being able to throw on just about anything and make it look stylish.

Although seeming to be casual about fashion or not too focused upon her looks or body shape, in reality the Sagittarius Glamazon can be extremely vain. Fortunately, she is born with the inner confidence necessary to carry herself well, and is not concerned with petty appearance details (unless there's some special occasion coming up). She can even feel quite comfortable being a few kilos over-weight (something that would unsettle other less confident signs), and although she may wish she hadn't gained quite so many extra inches, she won't necessarily have a stress attack worrying about these weight gains either. The Sagittarius Glamazon is more likely to go out and buy some looser clothes rather than make a big deal or become neurotic about her weight increase.

The Sagittarius Glamazon is a fun-loving individual. She has a great sense of humour, is usually good-natured and she thinks big, not small. Her friendships are many, she receives abundant invitations because people enjoy her company, and she generally marries very well. This all doesn't happen by accident. She is quick-minded and brilliant about making progress in her life and often forms very helpful and rewarding relationships with others. These associations assist her to advance up the success ladder of life. The Sagittarius Glamazon is often married to a millionaire, living the life that others dream about, or is in a position where she has built her own fortune. This hasn't occurred merely because she is a clever fashion package, which she often is; her advancement stems from her enormous lust for life and the enjoyment she provides to others when she is in their company. This star gal has got personality aplenty and this makes her one of the most popular Glamazons of the zodiac no matter what clothes she is or isn't wearing!

Sagittarius

Basic fashion style
Casually elegant.

Best fashion colour
Blues and silver.

Best fashion shoe
Comfortable pumps and ultra-high stilettos.

Must-have make-up item
Translucent powder for quick touch-ups.

Hair
Longish with highlights and special effects.

Hemline
Extreme (either really short or down to the ground).

Can't-live-without fashion accessory
Sunscreen (she's often an outdoorsy type).

Shopping habits
Erratic. The Sagittarius Glamazon has a great love for spending money, but she can also go on indulgent shopping sprees and then forget all about shopping for months.

Sagittarius fashion icons
Kim Basinger, Tina Turner, Jane Fonda, Bette Midler, Britney Spears, Tyra Banks, Christine Aguilera, Katie Holmes, Sinead O'Connor and Darryl Hannah.

The Capricorn Glamazon

The Capricorn Glamazon fits into two distinctly different fashion categories. She is either a style goddess or a queen of grunge. When she is the former, she is dressed to the nines; when she's the latter, she can get around in her raggedy jeans or gardening clothes almost every day. If she's into high Glama, and many Capricorns are, then she's most likely to be an established successful Glamazon, and when she's a Glama gal, whether she's in the boardroom making deals or in the bedroom making love, she's adorned in the right outfit. This gal of the zodiac usually knows what works for her and what doesn't, when it comes to fashion.

There are many Capricorn Glamazons who are ambitious, stylish, financially savvy and hardworking. These gals have their act together and often race up the ladder of success ahead of the other signs of the zodiac (and other Glamazons). And when Ms Capricorn Glamazon is climbing that ladder, generally she is wearing designer clothes, shoes and accessories. This gal knows how to look good and can be an expert at creating a fantastic fashion look. Generally she prefers crisp, clean fashion lines. She follows safe and traditional fashions rather than experimenting with funky trends. She is wise with colours and has a knack for mixing and matching garments with each other. Usually she has the perfect outfit for all seasons and occasions.

No matter what she has in her closet, the Capricorn Glamazon has the talent to morph one outfit into something appropriate to wear for whatever pursuit she is embarking upon next. She may accomplish this simply by adding a few accessories or doing something more drastic like altering the length of a hem.

Somewhat conservative, each Capricorn Glamazon has her own set of style boundaries that she doesn't like to cross. Very seldom is she a fashion victim. She avoids taking fashion gambles at all costs. Highly tuned in to her social position and status, she wants to fit in rather than stand out, and this desire to be 'correct' affects her shopping decisions. Designer labels appeal greatly to this sign and many Capricorns spend a lot of money on clothes. But while she can have expensive taste, as an earth sign the Capricorn Glamazon also likes to kick back in her tracksuit. When away from public scrutiny (possibly on weekends at her country home), nobody enjoys the luxury of languishing the hours away, resplendent in her cosy bathrobe or kimono, more than the Capricorn Glamazon.

Now not all Capricorn gals are interested in fashion or worried about style, but when a Capricorn is audaciously dressed or bold in her appearance, there is usually a sensible and well thought out reason for being so. She can be funky for a higher purpose—to fit in with a group of friends, to attract the attention of a certain mate, or to sell something or gain notoriety. Being very businesslike and money-minded, the Capricorn Glamazon will sometimes adopt a look or style that isn't truly 'her'. She will even wear something racy if she feels the occasion calls for it or it can profit her in some way.

Capricorn

Basic fashion style

She is the elegant social goddess of the zodiac. She dresses in sophisticated styles and leans towards comfort rather than trying to create a startling effect.

Best fashion colour

All the harmonious, pretty earth tones.

Best fashion shoe

Sensible and smart.

Must-have make-up item

Loads of moisturiser for the face and body.

Hair

Neat and sleek.

Hemline

Conservative.

Can't-live-without fashion accessory

Sun hat.

Shopping habits

Loves designer sales or showroom sample sales. Also loves buying things for the home.

The Aquarius Glamazon

What is the Aquarius gal of the zodiac likely to be wearing? Well probably the last thing you would expect her to wear. She can be extremely unusual in her choice of attire and she is not going to hide her fashion light under a bushel. She's a walking statement about her own fashion originality. Generally, she's interesting in her choice of attire, but that doesn't guarantee she will be stylish. It doesn't take designer dudes to make her feel fantastic; what makes her feel fantastic is 'being herself.' And being 'herself' opens up a huge range of fashion possibilities because no two Aquarians are alike or usually have anything in common—apart from their originality. She can be wearing dungarees or diamonds—you never can tell—and sometimes she'll wear them together.

When it comes to the way she puts her look together, generally it's more quirky than clinical. Fashionably unkempt is what many have to say about the Aquarius fashion package, and Aquarians of both sexes can be some of the most originally 'put-together' people on the planet. The Aquarius Glamazon has been known to break every fashion rule or trend imaginable. She also has an ability to wear odd socks, strange hairstyles, mix outrageous colours together or sport tattoos. So no wonder this gal of the zodiac is often the 'stand-out-in-the crowd' type, as she's likely to be dressed differently or styled in an original way. That aspect to her character can make her one of the most fantastic trendsetters of all. What gives her this original creative edge is her connection to the most unique and unorthodox planet of the zodiac, Uranus, the planet that rules her sign. However, whether she attracts attention or not, the Aquarius Glamazon is not likely to be intent upon creating a fashion style (unless it is her profession), because she doesn't need to. She already has her look—without even trying, it is her own.

Others may envy or attempt to imitate her look, but it usually doesn't work for them. The Aquarius Glamazon can sometimes be quite out of step with fashion because she can also be self-absorbed in her own world and fail to see what is going on around her. If you see someone walking down the street in the most peculiar outfit you have ever seen (looking like they've dressed in the dark and couldn't see what they are putting on, or they are stuck in the sixties), then they are likely to be an Aquarian! With this kind of originality, an Aquarian either looks like a style vision or a fashion disaster. The Aquarius Glamazon's personal style is something she chooses to either enhance or downplay, depending on her opinion about her appearance, and she will organise her clothes and personal style according to the life stages she is going through.

Aquarius

Basic fashion style

Their own individual stylish look. It doesn't matter as long as it is 'their look.'

Best fashion colour

All the shades of blue.

Best fashion shoe

Whatever is different and exciting.

Must-have make-up item

Glitter make-up (especially eye shadow).

Hair

The longer the better.

Hemline

Extreme lengths, from sweeping the floor with a mermaid's tail to the shortest of short butt skimmer.

Can't-live-without fashion accessory

Tweezers.

Shopping habits

She is a hopeless shopper who usually forgets what she went to the store to buy, and returns home with the opposite of what she was looking for.

Aquarius fashion icons

Christie Brinkley, Oprah Winfrey, Mia Farrow, Amber Valleta, Yoko Ono, Lisa Marie Presley, Cybill Shepherd, Heather Graham, Rene Russo, Farrah Fawcett, Vanessa Redgrave and Jane Seymour.

The Pisces Glamazon

Where is my costume designer? That's what every true Pisces girl needs—someone who can make her look like she's just stepped off a stage. She's the girl of dreams, so she needs to be a fantasy figure brought down to real life. In her heart, she is the zodiac gal who is always chasing rainbows, or believing in some fantasy or another. So what on earth does a Pisces gal wear to chase her rainbows? Something feminine and pretty of course!

Ruled by the planet of theatre, fantasy and illusion, Neptune, the Pisces Glamazon often lives a life that could be depicted on the screen as an incredible soap opera type drama. Her appearance and fashion style is greatly affected by the different stages or situations that her roller-coaster life takes her through. Relationships and romance run her life, so when she shops, subliminally she'll be attracted to outfits or styles that she senses may attract the right romance or man into her scene.

The Pisces zodiac princess never stops looking for her handsome prince, and she carries this dream of finding him in her heart for all her lifelong days. Because she is intensely emotional, the Pisces Glamazon will either be out partying all night, a huge success on the social scene; or doing the extreme opposite by sinking into one of her 'I need to be alone' withdrawal stages where she is struck by the Ivory Tower Syndrome and can't leave her bedroom. Much depends upon her emotional highs and lows. When she is in love, it seems as if she has the golden light of the universe radiating through her heart and soul (and she looks like a dream). When she's heartbroken or feels betrayed by others or life in general, she resembles a badly treated raggedy doll. The cycles of highs and lows this gal experiences effects her beauty, fashion sense, health and well-being enormously. So one glance in her direction quickly reveals how she is feeling right now. Of course, next time you look, she may have changed.

But because she is a dream-weaver and loves to create fantasies in her everyday life, many Pisces Glamazons set fashion trends and generate styles that others follow. She can be a wonderful make-up artist or stylist. She's an innovative thinker and therefore a masterful style creator. She is also extremely delicate, sensitive and emotionally geared, and her choice of clothing often seems to resemble a floating cloud or aura she wraps around herself. Because she feels life so intensely, many Pisces gals constantly battle with weight problems, gaining weight as a subconscious way to place a barrier or adorn armour to protect herself from the world (or even from herself).

Pisces

Basic fashion style

This gal loves fairy book fashion. She wants to dress in outfits that resemble everything from Little Red Riding Hood through to Cinderella.

Best fashion colour

Delicate shades and shimmers and silver and gold.

Best fashion shoe

The equivalent of a glass slipper.

Must-have make-up item

Lip liner.

Hair

Surreal style (feminine).

Hemline

Longish (like a princess).

Can't-live-without fashion accessory

Her credit card (which she regards as her modern day magic wand).

Shopping habits

Shopping is this gal's emotional outlet. But because she shops on a whim rather than with an organised approach, she often buys outfits that turn out to be white elephants.

Pisces fashion icons

Ivana Trump, Elizabeth Taylor, Cindy Crawford, Drew Barrymore, Vanessa Williams, Sharon Stone, Jennifer Love Hewitt, Niki Taylor and Liza Minnelli.

Your Glama Man by the Stars
Aries Glama Man

In love or lust

The first of the fire signs, Aries men are the zodiac's natural athletes. With his strong sexual desires that give rise to fiery passion when it comes to sex, this guy has the energy to keep up a passionate pace all night! However, the Aries man tends to run hot and cold with his ardour. When the flame of sexual desire dims with one gal, instead of trying to reignite it with her, he looks elsewhere to have it rekindled. Despite his macho image, he is sexually and romantically insecure and it takes the right, strong-willed woman to keep him satisfied and make him commit. He can be adept at holding back his emotions and affections.

Playing daddy

Although the responsibilities of fatherhood may weigh heavily on his shoulders, the Aries man is a true kid at heart and he gains enormous delight and satisfaction from his children. As much a friend as a father to them, he develops extremely close relationships with his offspring and often encourages them in sporting and outdoor pursuits. He has trouble dealing out discipline and often gets reprimanded—along with the kids—by mum!

On the job

He loves excitement and drama so any humdrum job filled with routine is sure to bring on a few migraines (his head is one of his physical weak spots!). On the other hand, if he has an exciting, entertaining job with lots of interaction with people, your Aries man will be a tireless, enthusiastic worker. He hates disappointment, delays or frustration, so he needs work that returns fairly instant rewards and praise or has a fat pay cheque to compensate for any hassles he goes through.

His not-so-nice side

He has a 'me, me, me' attitude. It is very easy (and even normal) for him to be totally self-centred. He can be alarmingly irresponsible and immature. His flippant manner often hides many deep-seated fears. He makes light of the things or areas of life that threaten him, rather than dealing with them and growing from the experience. The Aries man is renowned for his hot-headedness and impatience, so don't think you can rely on him all the time. When you need him most, he's likely to be missing.

What turns him on

What turns him on the most is 'himself'! He is his own universe in all kinds of ways and he will only invite you to share his world if he thinks you are worthy of a role in it. He's happiest when he's busy, but he also likes to be busy doing what he wants to do (he doesn't enjoy too much responsibility). The easier and more exciting the pathway his life flows along, the better. When the going gets tough the Aries man really isn't interested in suffering through the challenging times of life; and if he becomes besieged by other people's or life's demands, he is prone to 'head for the hills.' He craves easy-going relationships, especially in love. If you want him to love you, don't forget to pamper him and boost his ego; he likes to think of himself as the Greek god type; so humour him, overlook his short-comings, and he'll be yours forever!

Taurus Glama Man

In love or lust

Lookout! Some astrologers regard Mr Taurus as the most sensuous of all the lovers of the zodiac, but before you read on, be warned: this is one man of the zodiac who can tend to be hard to pin down when it comes to committing to marriage. And once he is married, he can be lazy about his lovemaking efforts at times. Ruled by the love planet, Venus, the sensual Taurus man is a true pleasure-seeker and this syndrome (indulging in wine, women/men and song), can be his main motivating force in life. But he usually enjoys being Mr Bachelor and he will wait patiently for Ms Right. It is only when he is 'in love' that he shows how romantic he can *really* be! In love he sometimes chooses someone who can take care of him (a mother type) rather than a girlfriend type. He doesn't like too many dramas in his romantic exchanges, so do not throw any tizzy fits around him—he'll dump you if you do.

Playing daddy

He's in his element around children because he assumes the responsibility of fatherhood very well. In fact, hidden beneath his 'I love bachelorhood' behaviour, lurks solid father material. Where other men might find a family life restricting, a mature Taurus guy forges inner strength and resilience from the responsibilities of fatherhood. He is a true provider and very protective of his children (especially of his daughters, who are usually beautiful examples of femininity). Although the kids might find him a bit tough on them at times (especially his sons), deep down they adore and respect him.

On the job

The Taurus man can be either a lazy beach bum or a borderline workaholic—all depends on whether he loves or hates his work. If he finds his work niche he can become a super-earner, but generally luck plays a big role in his work situation. He has a good business head on his handsome shoulders and if he is also blessed with enough ambition (depending on his individual chart), he can run his own business successfully. He enjoys his work…as long as he still has the time to have long lunches, play golf, surf…etc.

His not-so-nice side

He's the type who walks past a shop window and automatically can't help but check himself out in its reflection. If he's handsome (or even just mediocre looking), he can be totally in love with himself and that can make it hard to create a deep, lasting impression on him if you are trying to win his heart. He is weak-willed in certain areas of his character (the area differs from Taurus man to man), and needs constant bolstering or a push from others to get him going. As the beauty planet Venus rules his sign, Mr Taurus can be incredibly vain and selfish (he can even be a heartbreaker!). He is slow to anger but once he is—look out—he can really blow his top.

What turns him on

Indulgent living, great houses, fabulous yachts and an array of Barbie doll companions. He wants it all—money, fame, good looks, lots of attention and an easy road. Of course, he may not have these assets, but in his secret dreams he has them all. If he doesn't have an 'indulgent lifestyle' he can be a bully. Take any of these factors away and Mr Taurus feels emotionally unbalanced and has strange, undercurrents of depression or moodiness. Beauty, beauty and more beauty turns him on. Whether he finds it in an elegantly presented meal, a sleek car or a stunning woman, Mr Taurus adores 'pretty' things. He also needs to be able to express his own creative nature.

Gemini Glama Man

In love or lust

He's the chameleon man of the zodiac. One day he is an attentive, flirtatious and creative lover, the next you would swear he was living on another planet. Out of nowhere, he can become withdrawn and brooding. Mr Gemini's spontaneous erratic approach to life will have you guessing 'What's next?' Some gals adore this exciting twist to his personality while others loathe it, so you have to be wary when dealing with him. He's not a predictable kind of guy at all. His versatility and inventiveness, however, does make him a great sex partner and there is a definite kinky side to this zodiac male. He has a true 'twin' nature, so don't worry if it seems you have two lovers rolled into one. Just enjoy the surprise double package! Just don't rely on him coming back for more—he often is a one night stand!

Playing daddy

In many ways, playing daddy is Mr Gemini's easiest role in life. He is young at heart himself; and so once he gets into the swing of fatherhood (particularly when his children are old enough to communicate with him), he suddenly hits his stride. He is caring and protective. His children find it very easy to talk to him about 'kid's stuff.' He loves to play games with them, especially if the games are mental ones, so if he has the right kids, they often become best friends.

On the job

He's a go-getter when he finds his niche in the workplace. If he doesn't find his niche, he can sit around watching heaps of television and complaining about the lack of good jobs out there. However, there's a lot of creativity in this sign and Mr Gemini can be very artistic and versatile at work. Ruled by Mercury (the planet of the mind), his talents lie in communicating ideas and working with his hands. When he is in the right frame of mind he can have real moments of 'genius.' But because he loses focus quickly, short projects and tasks that don't require long spans of concentration suit him best. He thrives on working two (or more) jobs at the one time!

His not-so-nice side

Because of the 'twin' factor, Mr Gemini is often his own worst enemy. He says and does things he later regrets, and even though he says a lot, he often knows very little. The Gemini male is a verbal volcano just waiting to explode and sometimes when he gets on his high horse there is no way to shut him up! At times he is a downright gossip and trivia-monger. He can be tricky and deceitful in order to get what he wants. Surprisingly he can be obsessively jealous and can become vindictive if he feels others are operating against him.

What turns him on

He wants to be a go-getter, a global personality or a traveller. Mr Gemini loves interesting places, foreign people, challenging projects and learning new facts and figures. He hates routine or being bored. Keep him interested with charming and witty banter and by showering him with the latest electronic gadgets and bestseller books. Anything new and modern or experimental turns him on. He also loves being a social busy-bee—connecting with people is all-important in his world.

Cancer Glama Man

In love or lust

A Cancer man is not an easy man to deal with in a romantic relationship. He has many hidden quirks. Complex in character, he is sensitive, vulnerable and irrational. When you are involved with him in love and lust, don't expect constant reactions or responses both in and out of the bedroom! His moods can change in an instant. The 'mother' connection with Cancer is strong. Finding out how he relates to his mother is a likely indication of the way he is going to treat you. If he is infatuated with her and thinks she's the best person in the whole world, or he hates her with a vengeance, expect some of this to mirror in your relationship too. As a lover he is a surprise package and he can be super hot or very cold in the cot. His affections range from 'I love you' to 'I hate you', which can be exciting or annoying depending on your outlook.

Playing daddy

The Cancer male is father material all the way. From nursing tiny infants to preparing his children to spread their wings and fly the coop, Mr Cancer is a natural. He is one of the most family-oriented males of the zodiac and firmly believes that 'blood is thicker than water.' The experience of fatherhood can make him the happiest man in the world. He can also be a grumpy kind of dad—the kind that no child can please, if his life outside of the home isn't going to plan.

On the job

Although he has a contrary attitude to work (he goes through cycles of loving then hating his job), the Cancer male is often an excellent provider and very dedicated. In fact, many of the world's top business people and millionaires are born under this enterprising sign. Being self-employed also suits him—he can work his schedule around his ever-changing moods more easily than if he had a boss looming over his shoulders.

His not-so-nice side

Remember this guy can be prone to irrational, emotional behaviour. If he's had some heartbreak in his life, he can also be a hidden misogynist (a man who hates women). Just like there is a dark side to the Moon, the dark side to Mr Cancer can be very deep and mysterious. It is something seldom seen but when it does appear it can be awesome in its intensity. His personal problems often relate to women and his problems concerning his own sexuality. He is so tuned in to the feminine side of his own psyche that it can make him run away from female company or, at least, create the desire to punish them or himself. His periods of depression can scare people away. He can be mean-spirited and then he feels remorse about it, but his viciousness can spoil or damage a potentially good relationship over the long term.

What turns him on

He wants a feminine woman—somebody strong but supportive. If he's your dream man, give him plenty of reassurance and never ever criticise him or complain. When he is irrational or moody, ignore it and never mention it again. Be prepared to act like you are a devoted fan of his (and he can do no wrong) and he'll be yours for eternity. The Cancer male needs to be appreciated and complimented—often! When he truly believes he is loved (and has no doubt that he is loved unconditionally), he becomes the man of any woman's dreams. But be warned! He will put his lovers through plenty of tests in order to prove to himself that he won't be betrayed by someone of a flighty nature.

Leo Glama Man

In love or lust

Some regard him as the 'sperminator' of the zodiac. A fertile baby maker, he's a very sexy guy and often plays the sexual field more than most. He is born under the sign of the lion and the lion has its multi-sexual partners in nature. But that doesn't mean Mr Leo is not romantic. He's always looking for his one-and-only partner too (but once he finds her, whether he remains faithful or not is another question). There's a special connection between Leos and love. The heart comes under Leo's domain, so it isn't hard to see, astrologically, why Leo men make great lovers. Leo men thrive on romance and the more dramatic a romance the better. They know all about the trappings of love and romance—sending flowers, writing or reading poems, spicing up the passion and so on. Getting involved with a Leo man can send you soaring to new heights. It can also leave you nursing a broken heart. One thing is for sure—you'll never forget this love liaison!

Playing daddy

On the surface the Mr Leo appears to be a fabulous father, but the reality is that it can take years for him to truly enjoy this responsibility and paternal role. It often takes a lot of soul-searching before he can fully (and comfortably) express his fatherly nature. He best relates to his children when they are old enough to communicate with him on a one-on-one level. However, he is big-hearted by nature and will spoil them with his generosity and love. Being a sexual adventurer, he often has children by previous partners to cope with (and support) as well as attending his current brood. He can also continue to father children later in life!

On the job

Mr Leo is frequently a big success in the business world. The Leo male is, by nature, extremely ambitious and loves the high drama and theatrics involved in playing business and financial games. He usually finds his most fulfilling niche in life through his career (showing his talent at work is often the highlight of his self-expression). As a fire sign, he has plenty of energy and creativity to burn, so if he doesn't find the right career role, he suffers badly. His ego needs to be fuelled by success at work. He doesn't want to climb the ladder of success; he wants to soar up it.

His not-so-nice side

He's number 1! The Leo male is loyal, but when it comes to the crunch, his own self-preservation is his main game and he can be ruthless when anyone looks like taking something away from him that he doesn't want to give. This 'Mr Bossy Boots' can, in fact, be one-eyed and selfish. Just like his planetary ruler, the Sun, he thinks the world revolves around him. If too much compromise is needed to work out relationship problems, most Leo males would rather seek out greener pastures than stick around and give up something to make things work! At his worst, he will show you his 'love you and leave you' attitude (even if he doesn't intend to leave). He can be a very hard guy to manage, especially if he has a firm controlling grip over your heartstrings or your bank account.

What turns him on

If you want to please Mr Leo, simply treat him like a superstar, even if he is on social security. If he's a rich Leo, he'll expect you to run around after him, and love doing it too. Deep within every Leo male is the desire for fame and fortune (although not necessarily in that order!). He adores attention and dreams of having his name up in lights and often goes to extreme lengths to gain recognition and praise. He is aiming for the top and if you can help him get there, he'll love you for it! You'll have to show you've something special to offer to catch him—he only wants the best! Spontaneous adventure and wacky companions turn him on. He wants a love partner who is also a good friend, great companion and someone who can help him fulfil his own dreams.

Leo Glama Man

Perfect Glama buddy
> Sagittarius and Gemini.

Perfect Glama love match
> Aquarius, Aries and other Leos.

Famous Leo Glama men
> Mick Jagger, Bill Clinton, Antonio Banderas and Arnold Schwarzenegger.

Virgo Glama Man

In love or lust

Do not judge this guy by his appearance or behaviour. There are hidden sexual and romantic depths to every Virgo male that even the most observant woman can find difficult to comprehend. When it comes to love and romance, the Virgo male is a dark horse. He can be mild-mannered and shy like Clark Kent and then he can transform himself into Superman. This persona usually surfaces in emergencies or when he is alone with the object of his desire! On its highest level, love to him is magical, mystical and sacred, or alternatively, something he can totally live without! Sexually he is a passionate, lusty puritan. He has two attitudes to sex—one being love and romance and the other pure animal lust. In bed, and as a lover, this can be where his famous 'perfectionist' qualities show through!

Playing daddy

Usually the Virgo male is a terrific dad. He is a gentle but firm teacher and will spend hours helping his kids with homework and games that require attention to detail.

However, too often he expects his children to behave like sophisticated adults. He abhors noisiness, messiness and—eek!—changing nappies can make him sick to the stomach. There are also times when his Virgo mind is so overwhelmed with 'brain noise' that he feels too hassled to deal with his children. When these moods take control, he can become gruff and shut himself away with his bottle of headache pills and just wish the world would go away and leave him alone.

On the job

He frequently makes it to the top in whatever field he works in, but nevertheless he'll always be his own worst critic. Mr Virgo always thinks he should have, could have, done better than he has done in life. He's a natural worker and a perfectionist at heart. He has the rare ability of being able to combine creativity with brilliant organisational skills. He can annoy the Betsy out of his colleagues with his finicky habits and love of detail, but they are fond of him just the same—even though his workmates usually consider him to be a trifle wacky! However, because of his own specialised set of rules and routines, he is far happier working for himself.

His not-so-nice side

When the Virgo male is under extreme pressures or feeling betrayed, he can turn into a real Jekyll and Hyde character. The Virgo male is extremely complex— so intensely complex that many end up seeking out help from psychiatrists because they know they are slipping into dark thoughts too often. Those that don't analyse their responses put their many black moods or depressions down to the pressure of the outside world, rather than seeing them as problems that can be overcome within themselves. Nervous breakdowns, severe constipation, ulcers and insomnia are often experienced by the Virgo male. He can also be prone to compulsive behaviour.

What turns him on

He actually likes a quiet, good, quality life—not an exciting, thrill a minute existence. He can't take too much pressure, so peace of mind is vital to him. In relationships, loyalty, love and fairness are important values to the Virgo male and he is happiest when surrounded by a strong support team (this team may include his lover, work associates, friends, children etc). He must have everything running like clockwork. He loves helping people and when he is in tune with the world around him, he sees only the best in them (this is where his saint-like qualities come out). Be sexy, witty, clean, tidy, honest and accepting of his advice and he will love you forever! If he doesn't respect you, he'll torture you with his cool heart and uncaring attitude.

Virgo Glama Man

Perfect Glama buddy
Cancer and other Virgos.

Perfect Glama love match
Pisces and Taurus.

Famous Virgo Glama men
Richard Gere, Keanu Reeves, Lachlan Murdoch and James Packer.

Libra Glama Man

In love or lust

Just call him Mr Cool! The Libran man is regarded as one of the top heartbreakers and sex symbols of the zodiac. He is a super-smooth charmer and he adores wining and dining, romancing and dancing (particularly horizontally!) with the object of his sexual desire. In bed he is tender, sweet and sensitive. If you like a man to take his time, you'll love his creative approach to lovemaking. But because he has so many dewy-eyed female and sometimes even male fans, Mr Libra can sometimes be unreliable in matters of the heart (even the happiest married Mr Libra sometimes finds it hard to resist extra-marital flirtation). This is the love 'em or leave 'em guy of the zodiac, who often ends up with the girl with the biggest bank account or the biggest boobs.

Playing daddy

The Libra male considers himself to be a great dad, but at times when he has better things to do, he distances himself from his children without even realising it. This is because he usually has one foot inside the front door and another foot outside! He has a hectic social and business life and often breaks his promises to his children (he has been known to forget his children's birthday parties, graduations and other important events!) However, Mr Libra's heart is in the right place and generally he unreservedly adores his children. Lessons he teaches them are good manners, fairness and tolerance.

On the job

There are plenty of Libra men who are plain lazy and have no idea of what career path they want to follow! They are also often talked into careers that they aren't really interested in, such as taking over the family business, or working for his wife's father. But once the Libra male finds a satisfying job his many talents shine. Creative and ingenious, he has a flair for handling delicate business situations with diplomacy and his easy-going nature makes him extremely popular at work. He loves company and is at his best working with a diverse group of people (as opposed to solitary or shift work).

His not-so-nice side

He can turn out to be the greatest romantic rat of all the relationship signs. He doesn't like to be tied down and has unrealistic expectations of what relationships are all about. His desire is: 'If only the honeymoon would last forever!' Unfortunately for Mr Libra, it doesn't. He has a habit of heading for the hills the moment conflict or disharmony erupts (especially in love relationships). The Libra male can be the most selfish of all the zodiac signs. His lack of commitment can frustrate his companions and when he finally does make a decision, he tends to think only of himself. He can be inconsiderate about very important partnership issues and even become a lazy lover.

What turns him on

He is happiest when he has no problems in his world and feels that everybody adores him (whether he has earned this response or not!) He can't stand criticism or disharmony. What Mr Libra wants more than anything is an easy-flowing, care-free world and if he doesn't achieve this in a love relationship, sooner or later he will flee! He wants an ally, a special person who will be there when he needs them, someone who won't judge his shortcomings or complain about his inattentive behaviour. While he can forget you exist at times, if you ignore him, you've got an enemy on your hands. Shower him with attention and compliments and you'll get everywhere with the Libra man! He has extremely self-centred goals and desires, so if you can help him achieve these, you'll be a huge success with him. He often marries his boss's daughter or an heiress!

Libra Glama Man

Perfect Glama buddy

Other Librans and Sagittarius.

Perfect Glama love match

Gemini and Aquarius.

Famous Libra Glama men

Matt Damon, Guy Pearce, Luke Perry and Michael Douglas.

Scorpio Glama Man

In love or lust

He's the sexy, sizzle man of the zodiac. He is a deadly romantic type, in more ways than one. When he wants to, this man can fly you to the Full Moon and back. The 'right' Scorpio male can casually brush up against you and send shock waves through your cells, molecules and other areas too private to mention. Sexy Mr Scorpio can be your 'once in a lifetime' lover. If the chemistry works, neither of you will ever be the same again. There is nothing light or flippant about his style of romancing or lovemaking. Intense, sensitive and witty, the Scorpio male (if he genuinely falls in love with you), will stick by you through thick and thin, that is, unless overwhelming lust for someone else pulls him away. Scorpio men often have to battle against a very lustful nature.

Playing daddy

Scorpios are no ordinary dads. They well and truly rule the roost and everything else that comes within their control. Home life revolves around his moods, whims and wishes and when he is happy, his partner, children and friends are also likely to be ecstatic. But when he's down and depressed all hell breaks loose and his kids and everyone else will instinctively know to keep a low profile (be warned—he is usually much tougher and demanding on his sons than on his daughters!). Thankfully, his spells as a tyrant are short-lived. He is a softie at heart and is proud of his children's achievements.

On the job

He's got the potential to be a billionaire if he gets his business act together! Whatever it is a Scorpio takes on, he does it with a shrewd kind of passion or, alternatively, not at all! He sees things as black and white and tends to 'love' or 'hate' his job, colleagues and employer! However, when he feels passionate and happy about his career, he is a hard worker with plenty of ambition, dedication and long term vision. He is not too happy working for others, so usually ends up with his own business or in partnership with a friend.

His not-so-nice side

Read this carefully—don't mess with a Scorpio man or you'll be sorry. The dark side to Scorpio goes beyond the beyond! He is a secretive behind-the-scenes kind of guy. He doesn't talk about or acknowledge his feelings and he can be possessive and jealous, but you'd never even guess it. During these emotionally insecure phases, the Scorpio male uses his 'sting' like a weapon and he will say things that cut through you to your most sensitive inner core. He is quick to anger and slow to forgive. Think twice before getting on his not-so-nice side; he will make you pay for your real or imaginary 'sins' for eternity!

What turns him on

He's the control freak of the zodiac. He controls everything in his domain and what he can't dominate or manipulate he will either battle relentlessly (even if it kills him) or pull down an inner blind, pretending the situation or condition doesn't exist. If you want to please Mr Scorpio, love, obey and give him every reason to believe that he has the upper hand. He loves a woman who means what she says and says what she means, so don't try to deceive him because he will see right through your lies—no matter how small they are. If you go against him, he'll win!

Scorpio Glama Man

Perfect Glama buddy
Cancer and Taurus.

Perfect Glama love match
Capricorn and Virgo.

Famous Scorpio Glama men
Bill Gates, Leonardo Di Caprio, Matthew McConaughey, Ted Turner and David Schwimmer

Sagittarius Glama Man

In love or lust

The Sagittarian man is a sexual and romantic adventurer at heart, racing through the wild blue yonder often in search of his latest conquest. Mr Sagittarian also has a tendency to exaggerate and boast about his past and present sexual and romantic conquests. His reputation as a red-hot lover often stems from his own advertising, but he is very popular because he is outgoing, energetic and likeable. Often, this guy isn't one of the most faithful signs of the zodiac—far from it. Particularly in his youth, he spreads his sexual charms around. He can be the kind of lover who is 'here today, gone tomorrow!' But if he really does fall in love, and you'll know it—it can be the type of love that lasts forever. If you do find the right Sagittarian at the right time of his life, and you do fall in love, you can find yourself sharing a lifetime party together.

Playing daddy

He's a game player and he knows the secrets of the elixir of youth, so expect your Sagittarian man to be wonderful with children. He will always remain a 'big kid' at heart himself and he has just as much fun hanging out with his children as they do spending time with him. There is an element of the 'clown,' 'joker' and 'performer' in him that they adore, however, his many travels and adventures are likely to separate him from his children for long periods of time. He is also often the father of children from another marriage or involvement and can be busy working to keep up his child maintenance payments.

On the job

He can be the zodiac's most risk-taking entrepreneur. He often loves to do things that involve danger. He can be a big gambler too. If he has no other choice, he does have a knack for turning the most repetitious task or job into a challenge or adventure of some sort. The Sagittarian man is a super salesman usually found in advertising, politics, sport or travel associated industries. His optimism and enthusiasm make him extremely popular at work and he has a fabulous knack for combining business with pleasure! He usually has the gift of the gab too.

His not-so-nice side

Watch out! Getting involved with him (especially if he is one of the more flaky Sagittarian men around) can really mess up your life or empty your bank account. Mr Sagittarius can be very superficial. It is easy for him to break hearts, leave associates or employers in the lurch or mismanage his affairs so badly that other people come to grief as well. He isn't the most 'responsible' of the zodiac signs. He can also be extremely tactless and insensitive to other people's feelings—he is such an optimist that he shows no compassion to people proclaiming to be 'down and out'! He is self-absorbed and does what suits him, whether it is going to cause calamity or not to others.

What turns him on

He really wants everyone to like him. Being on top of the popularity stakes is a real turn-on, as he takes any fall from favour very hard. The Sagittarian male has a competitive spirit and he adores winning. Take him to a casino for the night, give him a sackful of free gambling chips and he'll be yours forever! Honesty and friendliness (and loads of forgiveness and understanding) are what he seeks in a woman. Trying everything in life (at least once!) is super-important to Mr Sagittarius and, to his credit, he is more than happy to give you the freedom to do the same.

Sagittarius Glama Man

Perfect Glama buddy
Leo and Aries.

Perfect Glama love match
Gemini and Cancer.

Famous Sagittarius Glama men
Brad Pitt, Don Johnson, Kiefer Sutherland and Brendan Fraser.

Capricorn Glama Man

In love or lust

No wonder Mr Capricorn's zodiac symbol is the randy goat! Beneath a façade that appears reserved and businesslike lies a man capable of giving a lot of love—and sexual excitement. He doesn't have trouble separating romance and sex and will often marry someone who isn't necessarily his ideal sexual partner, but who offers the right qualities as a partner and mother. Consequently, he sometimes has a secret mistress or girlfriend that nobody knows about. Because the Capricorn male feels a huge desire to be responsible and cautious in the outside world, the bedroom is his stage for really letting his hair down and going wild. He can be quite kinky at times. Flirtatious and sexually adventurous in his youth, Mr Capricorn can become less adventurous in maturity and can settle into marriage very well if he matches up with the right gal for him.

Playing daddy

He is a serious kind of guy and that's why the Capricorn male takes on the role of fatherhood with a bigger sense of responsibility and challenge that most other fathers. He wants only the very best for his children and he expects a lot from them. He goes out of his way to provide them with the ideal start in life, particularly where education is concerned. He is a true blue family man, but sometimes gets so caught up in this 'breadwinning' role (working back late and on weekends), that he spends very little time with his children. He teaches them the values of responsibility and commitment. He can be a tough dad to please!

On the job

This is where a true Capricorn man (the ambitious one) knows no zodiac equal. Work is as necessary to him as eating and breathing and many (although not all!) are workaholics! He is to be found amongst the world's leading entrepreneurs, company presidents, politicians, multi-millionaires and creative achievers. Ambitious, practical and reliable, he is a deep thinker who is prepared to work long and hard to reach his goals. The Capricorn male tends to make great friends with the people he meets through work. He often forms a sexual or longer-lasting relationship with someone he works with too.

His not-so-nice side

A worrier to an extreme, it can be hard to get Mr Capricorn to come down from the cross of his own creation. The Capricorn male has a complicated relationship with his mother and this can make him cautious of giving his heart and affections away to any woman completely. Because of his emotional insecurities (deep down he thinks he is the underdog of the world), he tends to surround himself with invisible emotional armour. He can go through deep bouts of depression. At his worst, he is mean with money and a notorious snob who judges people by their usefulness (i.e. whether they have money, status, prestige or good contacts).

What turns him on

Being in charge and proving himself as a success in the world. His ideals are to be a high achiever and have lots of sex (and most probably in that order). In love he desires a woman who will make him laugh, hopefully help him pay the bills, understand his high ambitions and give him daily doses of reassurance. Big business deals and stepping up the corporate ladder are also highly prized in his world. If he makes it to great wealth, he'll want to have a trophy wife to display as part of his worldly accomplishments.

Capricorn Glama Man

Perfect Glama buddy
Scorpio and Taurus.

Perfect Glama love match
Virgo and Aquarius.

Famous Capricorn Glama men
Denzel Washington, Mel Gibson, Pat Rafter and Nicholas Cage.

Aquarius Glama Man

In love or lust

If you meet him and you like him instantly, whatever you do, don't rush him. Give him some space. Mr Aquarius is the kind of man who likes to 'think' about love and sex before getting involved. If you want to steal his heart, keep in mind that

Mr Aquarius is more comfortable operating in intellectual, rather than emotional or physical zones. He is a wonderful friend and lover rolled into an unpredictable package. Once he stops worrying and relaxes, his fabulous knowledge of the latest and greatest sex positions, techniques, videos and manuals will surprise and delight you!

Playing daddy

Meet one of the most offbeat dads of the zodiac. His kids often cringe at his way-out jokes and clothes but really they adore their attentive, patient and 'hip' father. Straight-laced he is not! But no matter how much time he spends with his children the Aquarian dad still maintains a certain distance (although this seems to work well in building respect and cooperation around the home). He is an excellent mentor and teaches his children to have vision and goals for the future.

On the job

His planetary ruler, Uranus, rules electricity and Mr Aquarius is full of bright ideas! He is a highly original thinker and possesses a rare combination of discipline and creativity. He can be incredibly successful in business and he is always ready to try new solutions to old problems. He will often accept a role or position that others wouldn't as he can envisage the long term rewards and securities. On the down side, he thinks he knows more than everyone about everything. His favourite (most annoying) saying at work is, 'I told you so!'

His not-so-nice side

He can be cold and heartless. The Aquarian man can be very distant. He keeps his thoughts and emotions to himself to the point where those around him feel overlooked or neglected. He doesn't like to have flippant conversations and only wants to talk when he feels like it. It is easy to become lonely in his company when he gets out of phase. He doesn't trust people easily, but will probe and argue your beliefs and ideas in order to get to the bottom of your personality. He can be totally selfish and sometimes even calculatingly mean spirited.

What turns him on

A humanitarian by nature, Mr Aquarius has great empathy for the underdogs of life or anyone he feels has been dealt with unfairly. He wants to feel like he is one of the 'good guys' so he needs to be reassured that he is! He operates best with the solitude and space to think about his own thoughts and partake in his own (often weird) hobbies, musings or interests. The Aquarian man appreciates a woman who doesn't place too many high emotional demands on him. He is very worldly and a free spirit at heart. Give him a new cause or charity to get involved with and you'll pluck up his interest. Offbeat personalities fascinate him. He can be extremely bohemian or alternative in his outlook.

Aquarius Glama Man

Perfect Glama buddy

Libra and Leo.

Perfect Glama love match

Sagittarius and Gemini.

Famous Aquarius Glama men

John Travolta, Josh Brolin, Matt Dillon and Greg Norman.

Pisces Glama Man

In love or lust

He is the zodiac's knight in shining armour. The Piscean male loves to be in love and when you touch his heart, expect all the romantic trappings of courtship—flowers, love letters and gifts of sexy (even kinky) lingerie. Mr Pisces thrives on affection and he isn't shy about expressing his feelings. The more feminine you are, the more he will worship you. Kind-hearted and adaptable, love and lust play a big role in his life! Be warned though—Mr Pisces has been known to play the field with love and lust big-time! At worst, he can be two-faced and keep you dangling on his romantic string while he's busy courting some other gal you know nothing about.

Playing daddy

This guy suits the role of 'Mr Mum' more than most. Some of his finest qualities arise when Mr Pisces becomes a dad. He is supportive and sensitive although sometimes not entirely practical. His family is his security base but he is prone to moving this base according to his personal whims. He can propel his family into unusual living situations (like living on houseboats or moving overseas). He adores his children and is always willing to listen to their problems. A true softie, he would rather let his partner dole out the discipline!

On the job

Many Pisces men lack the ambition to work their way to the top. Competition threatens him and because he is so sensitive to his environment, the wrong working conditions can bring on headaches, and even bouts of depression. It is better for him to accept a job that he enjoys (even if the pay is lousy), than work for higher returns in a stressful position. He is often happier working for himself in a supportive, less pressured environment. He is extremely creative and imaginative.

His not-so-nice side

Because he operates under the influence of strange fantasies and desires, the Piscean man has several not-so-nice sides. He can lead a secret life, having habits or pastimes that those closest to him could never possibly imagine. Because he tends to believe his own lies (he talks himself into them), Mr Pisces can't always be trusted. He is so sensitive to the outside world that he often escapes through alcohol and drugs. He can be extremely difficult to deal with because of his irrational expectations of you and life in general.

What turns him on

His ideal dream would be to find a money tree and have a magic carpet ride through life. He isn't the kind of guy that wants to battle or struggle—he loves peace, harmony and happy days. He also needs a creative outlet for his talents, constant romance, lots of fantasy sex and a loyal, faithful and stable partner. If you cocoon him from the outside world and don't criticise him for his lack of ambition, he'll kiss the ground upon which you walk. He wants to live his dreams and he has many dreams to live!

Pisces Glama Man

Perfect Glama buddy

Capricorn and Scorpio.

Perfect Glama love match

Cancer and Virgo.

Famous Pisces Glama men

Bruce Willis, Aidan Quinn, Kurt Russell and Billy Zane.

'Don't just wish
upon a star...
be one.'

Athena

Chapter Twelve

CHARMED AND DANGEROUS

The 'females of the species' are canny creatures born with a natural intuition, and it is said that there's an enchantress in every woman. Well, if that's true, imagine how much power is forging inside a true, magical Glamazon! Your own Glama power, once harnessed and honed into peak condition, will always be there to help you get out of any sticky situation and ready to jump over any holes of despair. Here are some handy charms to introduce you to the realm of fun spells and sorcery-de-Glama.

Beauty and Love Spells

Everyone, even Glama girls, fret about the way they look. How about those bad hair days or when an angry pimple appears smack bang in the middle of your forehead or those dreaded 'I look fat in everything' days? When you feel low you will probably need some magical help to get you through those dreaded attacks of the fuglie uglies. Every time a modern woman applies her favourite red lipstick, whether it's from Yves St Laurent or Woolworths, or sprays her favourite Chanel, Gaultier or whatever glorious perfume she adores, she's following thousands of years of magic and love spelling. Because feminine magic and the tools of glamour go hand-in-hand and have always done so.

Magic rituals are incredibly self-empowering, and can work miracles for the way you look at yourself and how others see you. They can help you (and that studly Glama man you've had your eyes on) see through to the true power and beauty that is the real you. The key to casting successful beauty or love spells is to first learn to love and believe in yourself—that's what gives you the extra spark to bring out your charisma and true Glama power. But if you're feeling so low that you can't even get that together, just jump right in and start weaving the charm anyway. You'll soon find new found inspiration flowing through every cell of your being.

The best Moon times for love and beauty spells is either during a full or new Moon. It's simple to find some of the key ingredients for love spells—red and pink roses, divinely-scented gardenias, vines of jasmine and luscious chocolate. What you also need to do is enjoy the Sun and stars, collect pictures of love hearts, stock up on blush pink and the deepest of crimson ribbons, and rose quartz crystals and seashells—all powerful icons of sexual power. Create an altar to the goddess of beauty. Adorn your room with pretty mirrors, sculptures or posters of the goddess Venus and Aphrodite, blush pink and red candles and, whether your most magical scent is by Issey Miyake or a handmade ambrosia of Cleopatra, collect antique and new perfume bottles to store your gorgeous love potions and divine scents in because it's all magical, and it's all to do with the allure of feminine glamour.

Glamour Goddess

Empower your inner diva by creating this 'living' magical statue to ancient Glama. First thing you'll need to do is buy a statue or sculpture (any size or style that appeals to you) of either the goddess Isis, Venus or Aphrodite. Next you will need to collect these items of enchantment:

- three petals from either an orchid, lotus flower or pink geranium (plus extra)
- 30ml peach schnapps
- apricot or jojoba oil
- 1 teaspoon of chamomile flowers (or dried chamomile tea)
- 1 teaspoon of fresh or dried lavender.

Tear up the flower petals into small pieces and mix them together in a wooden or terracotta bowl. Pour in the peach schnapps and leave the mixture to settle overnight. The next day, pour in a cup of your chosen oil and place the bowl in front of your goddess statue. Sit quietly letting go of any negative thoughts and focus your mind on uplifting daydreams and feelings of joy and love. When you are ready, scoop up some of the oil with a teaspoon and pour it over the top of the statue as you say with conviction, 'Blessings to you Goddess of Beauty, you are me and I am you, together we shall be charged with the eternal power of the Universe.' Then lean over the statue and breathe near the face of the goddess as if you are breathing life into her and say, 'My breath shall be yours, and your breath shall be mine, we are now one goddess—together and divine.'

Complete your magical dedication by wiping the statue clean with a soft cloth and sprinkle the extra flower petals around her. Leave the statue somewhere in either your living room or bedroom and decorate the table she will sit on, to make an altar that will honour and cherish both the beauty of her goddess power and your own.

Whenever you are going out on an important date or need a boost of confidence, light a white or pink candle for a few moments in front of her and say, 'Beauty and love are mine, I am the Goddess divine.'

Magical Hair Glama

This is a spell to make your hair grow longer and faster. The best time to weave a Glama hair spell is on the day or evening of a Full Moon. You will need these ingredients:

- 1 candle
- 1 tablespoon of mayonnaise
- 1 tablespoon of champagne
- 1 teaspoon of olive oil (but if your hair is oily, substitute this with a teaspoon of lemon juice instead)
- a couple of tablespoons of full cream natural yoghurt.

At either midday or midnight, light the candle and then snip off a tiny piece of your hair with scissors (half an inch of just a few strands will do) and place the hair into a glass or china bowl. Next pour the champagne into the bowl and say, 'She who attends both wood and glade, I bid you here while this spell is made,' then stir in the mayonnaise along with either the olive oil or lemon juice and say, 'Diva of power hear my story, come enchant this crowning glory,' then mix in the yoghurt and dip your hands in the mixture and start applying the yummy mixture all over your scalp and hair right down to the ends. When all the mixture is on your hair say, 'And now that this spell has been cast, hear me now the magic will last.' Wrap your hair up with the towel and sit quietly and breathe calmly with the mixture left on for twenty minutes. When the time is up, wash your hair thoroughly with shampoo. If you must condition it afterwards make sure you use a very lightweight and non-greasy one.

Rosy Passion Potion

This is a powerful charm to attract passion and your sexy lover back into your arms. The ingredients you will need include:

- pinch of ground cinnamon
- pinch of allspice powder

- 1 cup white wine
- a red cloth
- three mature (already opened) red roses
- a piece of string.

Mix the cinnamon and allspice into the wine and let it stand under the sunlight (or near a window that gets the morning or afternoon sun) for at least an hour. Next dip your right index finger into the wine and trace a heart shape on the red cloth—don't worry if you can't see any shape, it is meant to be only visible to an expert sorcerer's keen eye. Focus passionate and sexy thoughts towards your lover to be, put the three roses on top of the cloth, roll it up and then tie the bundle up with the piece of string. Next walk outside or near an open window and leave everything to be charged overnight by the light of the Moon. The next morning, bury the rose bundle somewhere in the earth (or in a pot plant) near your front or back door. Soon the man of your dreams will be at your door.

When Only a Hex Will Do

There comes a time in every girl's (and guy's) life when a dose of real wizardry and wonder is totally called for—especially during those trying times when, despite all your best practical efforts and hard work, you just seem to be running on the spot and getting nowhere fast, or even worse, moving backwards in a downward spiral of hopeless negativity.

So, fear not, a solution is at hand. When all else fails, nothing quite beats a spot of conjuring and a boost of bewitchery, especially to protect you from those who may be intent on cramping your style.

The Ultimate Toad Test

You know the type—you don't have to turn this one into a toad because he already is one! He's that slimeball at work who just can't keep his hands to himself.

Not only that, he's real sneaky and nobody seems to know what's happening. This magic charm will fortify your own power to speak up and confront your enemy. As an added magical bonus, it can compel this cowardly cad to drop the charade and show his true slimy nature and toady side to everyone else. Before you bother using up valuable magical energy, see if he is worth the effort with this quick questionnaire:

1. Does he grope you or touch you unnecessarily?
2. Does he insult you in front of work colleagues?
3. Does he take the credit for work you've done?

If you answered yes to at least two of these questions, your enemy is definitely in line for a Glama hex. To cast the spell you will need:

- a piece of paper with his name written on it in black pen
- 1 clove of peeled garlic (or a teaspoon of garlic paste)
- 1 teaspoon of spring or mineral water
- 1 teaspoon of cod liver oil
- 1 teaspoon of dried rosemary
- a yellow feather (any kind of feather will do).

Place all of the ingredients into a jar and firmly twist on the lid. Shake the bottle for a moment while you say this incantation out aloud: 'With this elixir I now declare to repel the toad and reveal the lecher with good intent and for my welfare. If you touch me again, justice shall be here.'

The next day wrap the bottle in a plastic bag and take it to work with you in your bag or briefcase. At some stage during the day walk just once around your desk in a counter-clockwise direction while carrying the bag. (You can leave it inside your purse or briefcase if you like.) Finally, take the jar home with you that evening and bury the wrapped bottle in the ground somewhere near the front of your home. Leave it buried until the spell has worked its purpose. Afterwards you can dispose of the jar by throwing into a garbage bin.

Luck Bringer

This spell will banish any bad luck or negative energy out of your life. You will need to gather the following ingredients:

- a fresh ginger root or a teaspoon of bottled ginger
- some seaweed, straight from the sea if possible, but you can use seaweed from a nori roll or sushi paper (bought in health food stores or Asian food stores) or some canned or bottled seaweed.

The best time to perform this spell is at midday on any Sunday of the month. If your wish is to get rid of a jinx or when you think someone is sending you shadowy bad vibes, then cast this spell at noon on a Sunday. Find a pond or any stretch of water. Don't worry if you don't live anywhere near a water source such as a river, the sea or a lake, just use your imagination. A swimming pool or a filled sink or bathtub sprinkled with a touch of salt will do. Go stand near the water whilst holding the ginger and either the nori paper or seaweed in your right hand. Breathe calmly and relax for a minute while you try to focus your mind on peaceful and serene thoughts. As you gaze into the water, repeat this incantation: 'By the Gods of the wind and sea, ill wind and conflict is banished and sent far away from me.'

Throw the ginger and seaweed into the water, then close your eyes and imagine that you are strolling along a beach, a warm breeze blowing through your hair, having a great time and feeling completely refreshed and untroubled and free of worries. Wind up the final power of the spell by saying with confidence and conviction in your voice: 'Now I see reflected only serenity and affection. And so it is, it is so. And so mote it be!'

If you have used a bathtub or a sink for the spell, pull out the plug and let all the water drain out. Then throw away any leftover ginger or seaweed.

Barbie's Revenge

She's got bedroom eyes and a hairstyle to match. Her theme song is 'You're So Vain.' She's as shallow as an empty swimming pool and she's after your man!

Quick! Do yourself a big favour! For the sake of your relationship and for the 'good of all,' it's time to brew up this, 'Hey girl, what the hell happened to your hair?' spell.

It's harmless but works like a charm to ruin the scarlet temptress' fun, and to give any other potential home wreckers second thoughts. The magical ingredients you need are:

- 1 teaspoon of salt
- 1 doll (preferably one that has been used or bought from a second-hand store
- 1 or 2 dog hairs
- 1 tube of eyelash or nail glue
- a mirror.

The best time to cast this spell is at midnight. Find a quiet space where you can perform your magic ritual and place all your ingredients onto a table or on the floor. Begin your spell by sprinkling a circle of salt on the floor around you in a clockwise direction. Next, hold the doll in both hands and say, 'I cast this spell in the name of good, no harm will be done.' Next, stick the dog hair onto the head of the doll with the glue and let it dry for a few moments. Then, take the doll and sit on the floor inside the circle of salt. Meditate for a few moments and then say these magical words: 'When you look in the mirror, you'll catch sight of your foul deeds, when my lover sees you next he'll know it's me that he needs. Step back from your self and look into the light, your hair will be a fright, but your soul will be right.'

Next place the doll in front of a mirror and leave it there all night and the next day until you know that it's served its magical purpose. When you know that the spell has done the trick, pull off the dog hairs from the doll, throw them in the bin and sprinkle the doll with a bit of salt to cleanse it. Then wash the doll's hair in some spring water, towel dry and, voila! Your doll can be put back into its proper place (along with your husband).

Stalker Stopper

This spell is for any creepy girl or guy who is sending you nasty emails or is harassing you on your phone. Apart from all the obviously essential legal back-ups, and having your phone number and email changed, this ritual helps give a magical boost to any practical anti-stalking steps you're gonna take. The best time to weave this spell is on a Saturday or the night of a Full Moon. Beforehand, you will need to gather:

- a piece of brown paper (from a grocery bag is fine)
- 1 black pen
- a piece of a spider's web—a real one is great or you can also buy the party store variety that's used a lot at Halloween. It can be either canned, paper or plastic
- some clean kitty litter (before Kitty's used it, of course!)
- a litter tray.

Write the creepy stalker's name on the piece of paper with the pen and then wrap it around the spider's web and place it in the bottom of the litter tray and pour enough kitty litter on top to cover everything. Next, allow yours, or a friend's kitty, to use the litter as per usual, and when the tray is dirty enough (the cat will be sure to tell you when it is), throw the dirty litter and paper in the garbage. The tray can be put back to every day use by just washing it out with warm soapy water. And please don't forget to thank good ol' kitty for a job well done! Only visible side effects are possible fits of laughter (you, not them), and occasional coughing up of fur balls (the stalker, not you).

Spy Detector

Got the feeling there's a traitor in your midst? Something smells in the State of Denmark but you just can't put your finger on who's the rotten egg? To help expose spies and disloyalty, cast this spell on the first or last Saturday of any month. You will need:

- an indoor or outdoor clothesline
- 1 wooden clothes peg
- 1 black pepper shaker
- any photographs of the people you suspect.

Pin the photographs on the clothesline with the wooden peg and then stand close by. Sprinkle the pepper around yourself in a counter-clockwise circle as you say these words out loud: 'Gossip depart, pretence retreat, treachery is now revealed. Each lie you utter shall come back to you, no more shall you betray the just and true. And so it is, O blessed be.'

Next leave the photographs there overnight to be charged by lunar energies (you can wrap the photos in a plastic bag or cling wrap if you are concerned about rain), and clean up any leftover pepper. The next day unpin the pictures, throw away the clothes peg and place the photos inside a brown paper bag. Then place the bag in a safe place where it will not be disturbed and leave it there for as long as it takes the spell to work. The spell's energy will last up to three months. Anytime after the spell has performed it's magical duties, you may unwrap the photos, throw away the paper bag and sprinkle any wanted photos with salt to cleanse and purify them, so you can safely put them back in their usual place.

And so girls, it seems our job is done. We've given you essential tips and witty quips to give you the winning edge. So now, Glama graduates, venture out into the world and spread your own brand of style and glamour into the universe. And remember, as our good friend Ivana always says, 'Darlings, in my vocabulary, there's no such thing as casual.'

'Magic is believing in yourself, if you can do that, you can make anything happen.'

Johann Wolfgang von Goethe

Athena Starwoman

A dedicated fashionista with a quirky cosmic style of her own, Athena is well-known internationally as one of the world's leading astrologers. Athena's regular zodiac columns appear in *Vogue* (USA), *The Australian Women's Weekly* (Australia), *Star Magazine* (USA), *Life & Style* (Greece) and *Elegance* (Holland). She has also written the astrology books *Zodiac*, *Zodiac Lovers* and *Soulmates and the Zodiac* plus a magical spell book entitled *How to Turn Your Ex-boyfriend into a Toad*, in conjunction with her friend, Deborah Gray.

Married to American inspirational speaker, Dr John F Demartini, both Athena and John lead a jet set gypsy existence commuting from John's head office in Houston, Texas to their 'temple-like' penthouse on the Gold Coast of Australia. Always on the go, the two of them are either exploring or returning to somewhere special around the globe. Since it's launch in Oslo in March 2002, Athena now calls the luxury residential ship *The World* her home. Residing in an apartment on board, she sails into New York, Monte Carlo or the wonderlands of Iceland, St Petersburg or Alaska, writing her columns and books on the seven oceans of the world.

Athena says: 'As a child from a working class family in Melbourne, I dreamed of living a full and glamorous international life. Back then, it certainly seemed impossible, but magically now I live that life! Within the pages of *Glamazon*, Deborah and I detail our Glama secrets to you. My hope is that these insights will assist you to succeed and excel on your own journey de Glama. Go out and live your dreams!'

Deborah Gray

Former fashion model Deborah Gray, may be known nowadays as an acclaimed author, but Deborah's first career was in politics. She worked as a junior secretary (a glamorous one, of course!) to a Prime Minister, but that quickly changed after winning a teen modelling competition at fifteen years of age, and she was signed by Australia's leading agency at the time, soon after becoming a highly successful model in fashion magazines and television commercials. Deborah further developed both her singing/songwriting skills (she is an award-winning songwriter after winning the 1998 Bronze Medal in an international songwriters' contest) and became a versatile comedic and dramatic actress on Australian television. She has starred in shows such as 'The Young Doctors', 'Catch Us If You Can', 'Bellamy' and 'The Best of Friends'. Deborah has toured the world writing music for Olympic ice skaters Torvill and Dean as well as fulfilling recording contracts and singing assignments in some of the world's most legendary Jazz venues (Maxim's, Supper Club, Blue Note).

Deborah is now Australia's best-selling magickal author and is acclaimed world-wide as one of the most successful writers of her genre. Her inspirational words have been translated into ten different languages, including German, French and Japanese, and continue to excite the imaginations of her many thousands of readers and fans around the world.

She has written six internationally best-selling books including *The Nice Girl's Book of Naughty Spells*, *How To Be a Real Witch*, *Good Witch's Guide to Sexy Sorcery*, *Spells for All Seasons* and co-authored *How to Turn Your Ex-boyfriend into a Toad*, which caused a sensation with its runaway success and breakthrough cutting edge approach. Deborah is an inspirational speaker, writer and producer, whose internationally recognised expertise, graceful features and ability to entertain is sought after on international television and radio, seminars and popular talk shows such as 'Today', 'Good Morning Australia' and 'Kerri-Anne Kennerley'. Currently, Deborah is recording a follow-up to her highly acclaimed 'Jazz Fresh' CD and is writing and producing an exciting new television program to be launched around the world in 2004.

INDEX